MILK & CARDAMOM

Spectacular Cakes, Custards and More,
Inspired by the Flavors of India

HETAL VASAVADA

founder of Milk & Cardamom

PAGE STREET
PUBLISHING CO.

PAGE STREET
PUBLISHING CO.

First published in 2019 by
Page Street Publishing Co.
27 Congress Street, Suite 105
Salem, MA 01970
www.pagestreetpublishing.com

Distributed by Macmillan, sales in Canada by The Canadian Manda Group.

24   23   22   21   20   2   3   4   5   6

ISBN-13: 978-1-62414-774-6
ISBN-10: 1-62414-774-7

Library of Congress Control Number: 2018961278

Cover and book design by Molly Gillespie for Page Street Publishing Co.
Photography by Hetal Vasavada

Printed and bound in the United States

DEDICATION

To my sweet baby girl Elara. I promise to always let you lick the frosting off the whisk and show you the same magic of Indian desserts that my mother taught me.

To my husband, Rhut, you are the spark that ignited my passion and helped me turn it from a hustle to a career. I love you.

TABLE OF CONTENTS

BREADS & JAMS   135

DRINKS   155

 INTRODUCTION

Growing up as a first generation Indian-American, I often yearned for the same experiences my friends had. Baking cookies with their grandmothers, frosting cupcakes for birthday parties or simple things like licking brownie batter off a spoon were experiences I wanted so badly. Like most Indian-American kids, I wanted every other food but Indian food. I dreamt of stuffing my face with cookies and cakes, but instead got Parle-G biscuits and sweetened semolina pudding. As a child, I remember promising myself that when I grew up I would bake cookies with my kids and let them lick the frosting out of the mixing bowl.

What I did get were mornings filled with chai and biscuits, holidays like Diwali where I sneakily smashed all the ladvas (also known as laddoos) to find a lucky coin and warm summer afternoons spent with my grandmother where we'd quietly sit next to each other enjoying an ice cold kulfi. Indian desserts (mithai) were usually eaten during special events. Boxes and boxes of mithai would be sent to families during religious holidays, weddings or family gatherings. Every sweet I have brings me back to a special memory or moment.

It wasn't until I was older that I realized how special my memories were and how they were so closely connected with the food I had tried so hard to avoid eating. It wasn't until I moved across the United States, from New Jersey to San Francisco, that I realized how much I missed those sweets. I spent hours video chatting with my mom trying to translate her "finger's worth of ginger"-style notes into an actual measured and replicable recipe.

As my love for food and its ability to bring people together grew, I found myself in the kitchen experimenting more often. My first experience baking was through boxed mixes and canned frosting. When I got to college and started studying organic chemistry, I learned the role of each ingredient and the importance of the techniques used in baking from scratch. There is a method to the madness, and every movement in the process of baking has a reason behind it. I started manipulating the ingredients and techniques to create desserts with unique flavors and textures like the ones you will find in this book.

Later on, I started taking pieces of my American childhood and mixing them with my Indian upbringing, creating dishes that represented me. Not quite 100% American and not fully Indian. I decided to take one of my creations and try out for a cooking show hosted by the famous Gordon Ramsey, *MasterChef*. Somehow, I managed to make it onto the show with my Indian-style apple pie made with Indian spices and a cardamom whipped cream.

Throughout the show I continued to share dishes that defined my upbringing with American twists. Little did I know that there was a whole generation of Indian-Americans who could relate to me and my food story. There were thousands of people who grew up on cardamom-spiced shortbread cookies (nankhathai) but also ate their weight in chocolate chip cookies.

These recipes are close to my heart. I dreamt them up while going through the food memories of my childhood and the memories I want to create for my daughter as she grows up. Like everything I do, I completely threw myself into this project. I wanted to learn more than just my mother's recipes—I wanted to know where these desserts originated and how they came to be. In the process, I figured out shortcuts and mastered the techniques of making various Indian desserts, and now I can share them with you!

In this book, you'll find recipes that are brand new and unique and some that are traditional. I always struggled with being "too American" or "too Indian." Luckily with food there is no right or wrong. Are these recipes totally authentic? No. Are they still amazingly tasty and do they remind me of the Indian desserts I grew up with? Yes. I hope you go through this book and learn about Indian desserts, their history and the stories attached to them.

lutal

CREAMS, CUSTARDS & PUDDINGS

Most kids grow up with memories of licking batter off a spatula while baking with their parents. My childhood memories consist of me licking saffron-scented shrikhand off my fingers and savoring every bite of a pista kulfi in the parking lot of the Patel Brothers after long Indian grocery shopping trips. I can almost taste it now, freshly ground cardamom and crunchy pistachios all swirled with rich full-fat cream!

It's all about creams, custards and puddings in an Indian home, not so much about cookies and cakes. Most homes in India aren't equipped with ovens, but they all usually have a stove, refrigerator and, if you're like my family, a cow! Whenever I would visit India, we would get fresh cream from the cow when making any sort of custard or pudding.

Many of the puddings in India are made of various toasted flours. The first sweet dish I ever had was a semolina-based pudding called seero, which is made with ghee and lightly sweetened with sugar. My mom would make it for me when I had a sore throat since it was slick with ghee—the panacea to all ailments, according to my mother.

The dishes I share in this chapter like Kheer (Rice Pudding with Roasted Grapes, page 27), shrikhand (Shrikhand Parfait, page 16) and Seero (Semolina Pudding, page 12) were always made at home. I wanted to take comforting home-cooked dishes and tie them in with rich desserts like crème brûlée, panna cotta and pot de crème. In some cases, I took traditional dishes like kheer and added a Western twist to them! I wanted to create desserts that I, as an Indian-American, could identify with. Using flavors that my mother and her mother and so on used in traditional Indian desserts and transferring them into the American recipes that I was experimenting with opened up a whole new world of possibilities in my kitchen (and now yours too!).

SEERO (SEMOLINA PUDDING)

This recipe is the real OG. Also known as sooji ka halwa, it's the first sweet most Indian kids have, and is served as a prasad (blessed food), a breakfast accompaniment or a simple dessert after a meal at home. Seero is also the first sweet my daughter ever had when she was a baby. It has a soft, buttery texture with a nutty flavor that comes from the toasted semolina. My version doesn't have much sugar, so feel free to increase or decrease the amount of sugar to your liking.

MAKES
4 TO 6 SERVINGS

1 tbsp (8 g) shelled raw pistachios

1 tbsp (9 g) raw almonds

1 tbsp (9 g) raw cashews

¼ cup (50 g) granulated sugar

1 cup (240 ml) water

¼ cup (55 g) ghee (see Note)

½ cup (84 g) semolina

Toast the pistachios, almonds and cashews in a small nonstick skillet over medium heat for 4 minutes. Pour into a bowl to cool. Once cool, chop the nuts coarsely and set aside.

In a small saucepan, add the granulated sugar and water. Dissolve the granulated sugar in the water over medium heat. Once all of the sugar has dissolved, set aside.

In a nonstick skillet, add the ghee and semolina. Cook the mixture over medium-low heat for 4 to 5 minutes while stirring. The semolina will turn light brown and give off a nutty fragrance. Pour the granulated sugar water into the semolina and turn up the heat to medium-high. Let it sit for 1 minute without mixing. The semolina will soak up all of the water and thicken. Stir for 1 minute and then spoon into the serving bowls. Top with the toasted chopped nuts and serve while warm or at room temperature.

NOTE: Ghee is a type of clarified butter where all the milk solids have been removed. It has a high smoke point and is used in lieu of oils and butter in Indian cooking. You can use store-bought ghee or make it yourself at home by adding 2 pounds (907 g) of good quality butter to a large saucepan over medium heat, and simmering until it turns golden yellow, about 8 to 10 minutes. Once the milk solids float to the top into a white foamy layer, strain it through a couple layers of cheesecloth into a jar and cool. It'll keep for a year in the refrigerator. I also like to make Brown Butter Ghee (page 96) which has a nuttier, richer flavor that's perfect for making sweets with.

HALDAR NU DOODH PANNA COTTA

The moment the golden milk trend went viral, my mom gave me a call to tell me, "I told you so." I spent YEARS being tortured with haldar nu doodh on a nightly basis. My mom believed turmeric could cure just about every ailment there was. Sprained knee? Turmeric. Pimple? Turmeric. Sore throat? You guessed it . . . turmeric. The only way my mom could get me to drink it was to add cardamom, saffron and a little bit of sugar. Now that I'm older, the taste has kind of grown on me.

MAKES
4 SERVINGS

HALDAR NU DOODH PANNA COTTA

2 cups (480 ml) heavy cream

1 tsp turmeric powder

¼ tsp ground cardamom (see Notes)

Pinch of saffron

2 tbsp (30 g) granulated sugar

½ tsp agar agar powder (see Notes)

MACERATED PEACHES

¼ cup (96 g) peaches, ¼-inch (6-mm) dice

1 tsp granulated sugar

½ tsp honey

CARDAMOM WHIPPED CREAM

¼ cup (60 ml) heavy whipping cream

½ tbsp (4 g) powdered sugar

Pinch of ground cardamom

½ tbsp (4 g) shelled roasted unsalted pistachios, thinly sliced

To make the haldar nu doodh panna cotta, add the heavy cream, turmeric, cardamom, saffron and sugar into a heavy-bottomed saucepan over medium-high heat. Whisk well and bring to a boil, then simmer on low. Whisk in the agar agar powder and simmer over low heat for 2 minutes while continuously whisking. Pour the cream into four 4-ounce (113-g) ramekins or a mold. Cool and refrigerate for at least 2 hours or overnight. If you used a mold, just gently pop the panna cotta out of the mold and place onto your serving plate.

When you're ready to serve, toss the diced peaches with the sugar and honey in a small bowl, and set aside for 10 minutes.

While the peaches are macerating, make the cardamom whipped cream. Add the heavy whipping cream, powdered sugar and cardamom to a small mixing bowl. Whisk the cream until it reaches soft peaks, about 4 to 5 minutes.

To serve, top each panna cotta with macerated peaches, a dollop of cardamom whipped cream and a sprinkle of sliced pistachios.

NOTES: All of the recipes in this book utilize green cardamom. You can find green cardamom in three forms: whole pods, whole seeds and powdered. In many recipes I call for cardamom seeds that are freshly ground. You can grind the seeds using a mortar and pestle or a coffee blender. Freshly ground spices give the desserts an extra kick and the cardamom flavor is at the forefront of the dish. For dishes where I want a mellower flavor, I use ground cardamom. You can find cardamom seeds at your local Indian store or online.

This recipe uses agar agar powder instead of gelatin since gelatin is not vegetarian. You can find agar agar powder at your local Asian grocery store or on Amazon.

SHRIKHAND PARFAIT

Shrikhand has to be one of my favorite dinner party desserts! It's mostly found in the Western states of India and is made of hung curd, a thick and creamy drained yogurt. It's similar to Greek yogurt but 100 times creamier and thicker. It's typically flavored with saffron and cardamom, and if you're feeling fancy, you can add mango purée or rose water to it! I changed up the original recipe to add more textures to the dessert. Crunchy cookie crumbs, juicy fresh mango, fluffy whipped cream and thick shrikhand—all in one bite!

MAKES
8 (8-OUNCE [227-G]) PARFAITS

SHRIKHAND

3 cups (680 g) plain Greek yogurt

½ tsp saffron

½ tbsp (8 ml) warm milk

¼ cup (30 g) powdered sugar

½ tbsp (3 g) cardamom seeds, finely crushed

¼ cup (30 g) unsalted shelled pistachios, chopped, plus more for topping

1 tbsp (8 g) charoli seeds or pine nuts, plus more for topping

24 speculoos cookies (I prefer Biscoff)

½ cup (82 g) mango, ¼-inch (6-mm) dice

VANILLA WHIPPED CREAM

2 cups (480 ml) heavy whipping cream

¼ cup (30 g) powdered sugar

2 tsp (5 g) vanilla bean paste or extract

To make the shrikhand, place a strainer over a bowl. Cover the strainer with 3 layers of cheesecloth. Pour the yogurt into the cheesecloth. Pull up all of the corners of the cheesecloth and twist it tight. Place a plate and a heavy jar or can on top of the cheesecloth. Refrigerate for 8 hours.

The next day, add the saffron to the warm milk and let it bloom for 5 minutes. Remove the yogurt from the cheesecloth and place it into a medium bowl. Whisk in the powdered sugar, bloomed saffron and milk, and cardamom. Whisk until well incorporated. Place plastic wrap directly onto the surface of the yogurt and refrigerate for 4 hours.

While the shrikhand is resting, toast the pistachios and charoli seeds in a skillet over medium heat for 3 to 5 minutes, or until fragrant. Once done, pour into a bowl and set aside to cool. Add the speculoos cookies to a blender and pulse until you have coarse crumbs and set aside.

After the shrikhand has rested, whisk the shrikhand for 2 minutes so it's nice and fluffy. Spoon the shrikhand into a piping bag and snip off the tip of the bag so there is a 1-inch (2.5-cm) opening. Set aside.

To make the whipped cream, add the cream, sugar and vanilla to a large cold bowl. Use a hand mixer to whip the cream on high for 5 minutes, until it forms stiff peaks. Spoon into a piping bag and snip off the tip of the piping bag so there is a 1-inch (2.5-cm) opening. Set aside.

To assemble the parfait, spoon ¼ cup (21 g) of the speculoos cookie crumbs into the bottom of each cup. Pipe about ¼ cup (57 g) of shrikhand on top of the cookie crumbs. Spoon 1 tablespoon (11 g) of mango on top, and then fill with whipped cream. Sprinkle the chopped pistachios and charoli seeds on top. Refrigerate until you are ready to serve.

NOTE: There are two types of cardamom, green and black. Black cardamom is dried over a fire pit, giving it a smoky, savory flavor. Green cardamom is picked before the plant reaches maturity and is sold as is, without any processing. The light floral, vanilla-like flavor of green cardamom is found in almost every Indian dessert. I like to think of it as the vanilla of India!

NO-CHURN MANGO KESAR PISTA KULFI ICE CREAM

Kesar pista ice cream was the only reason I ever agreed to go on long trips to Patel Brothers Indian grocery store in Edison, NJ, growing up. I hated going Indian grocery shopping with my parents; it took forever, and I just wanted to spend my weekends playing with my cousins. To get us out of their hair, my parents would buy my sister and I kesar pista (saffron and pistachio) kulfis to enjoy in the parking lot while we waited for them.

In this recipe, I added kesar mango purée, which you can buy at the Indian grocery store. If you don't have one nearby, you can blend up an Alphonso mango.

MAKES
1 QUART (946 ML)

1 tbsp (15 ml) whole milk

1 tsp saffron

1¼ cups (300 ml) heavy whipping cream

⅔ cup (160 ml) sweetened condensed milk

½ cup (120 ml) mango purée

¼ tsp salt

⅓ cup (41 g) shelled pistachios

Warm the milk in a small saucepan or a microwave until it is lukewarm, about 10 seconds. Add the saffron, stir and set aside. In a large mixing bowl, add the heavy whipping cream and whisk on high for 3 to 4 minutes until it forms soft peaks. Add the sweetened condensed milk, mango purée, saffron milk and salt, and whisk on high for 5 minutes. Coarsely chop the pistachios and fold into the ice cream mixture. Pour the mixture into a container, cover and freeze overnight before serving.

GINGER-CHAI CHOCOLATE POT DE CRÈME

Adhraak chai (ginger chai) is my mom's version of chicken noodle soup. If I was sick, I was getting a hot cup of ginger chai with a side of Parle-G biscuits to help soothe my throat and make me feel better.

For an authentic cup of chai, you should buy the cheapest black tea you can find, also known as CTC (crush, tear, curl) black tea. It is the main type of tea used in India. CTC black tea has a slightly bitter taste that pairs really well with the dark chocolate and ginger.

MAKES
6 (4-OUNCE [113-G]) RAMEKINS

GINGER-CHAI CHOCOLATE POT DE CRÈME
¾ cup (200 g) dark chocolate (75%) morsels

2 cups (480 ml) heavy whipping cream

⅓ cup (80 ml) whole milk

4 tbsp (20 g) black tea (preferably CTC)

2 tbsp (5 g) minced ginger

½ tsp ground cinnamon

½ tsp ground cardamom

¼ tsp ground cloves

¼ tsp ground nutmeg

2 star anise pods

½ tsp salt

6 large egg yolks (see Note)

½ cup (100 g) granulated sugar

1 tbsp (7 g) cocoa powder

2 tbsp (8 g) candied ginger, chopped, optional

WHIPPED CREAM
¼ cup (60 ml) heavy cream

½ tbsp (4 g) powdered sugar

½ tsp vanilla extract

Preheat the oven to 300°F (149°C).

Add the chocolate to a microwavable bowl and microwave in 15-second increments, stirring between each increment, until all of the chocolate is melted. Alternatively, if you don't have a microwave, set up a bain-marie by bringing a small pot of water to a boil and placing a small bowl on top of the pot, making sure the bowl does not touch the water. Add the chocolate to the bowl and stir until melted.

In a medium heavy-bottomed saucepan, add the heavy whipping cream, milk, black tea, ginger, cinnamon, cardamom, cloves, nutmeg, star anise and salt. Bring the cream to a simmer over medium heat. Remove from the heat and cover. Let the cream steep for 10 minutes, then strain it into a medium bowl. Whisk in the melted chocolate and set aside.

In a separate bowl, whisk the egg yolks and granulated sugar for 5 minutes, or until pale and fluffy. Slowly pour the chocolate and cream mixture into the whipped egg yolks while continuously whisking. Strain the mixture into a large measuring cup or pitcher.

Divide the custard into six (4-ounce [113-g]) ramekins. Place the ramekins in a 9 x 13–inch (23 x 33–cm) baking pan and fill the pan with water until it comes halfway up the sides of the ramekins. Cover with foil and bake for 30 to 45 minutes, or until the center is barely set and wiggles a little when gently shaken. Cool and chill the pot de crèmes in the refrigerator for 4 hours.

When ready to serve, make the whipped cream by whisking the heavy cream, powdered sugar and vanilla in a small bowl until it forms soft peaks. Dust each pot de crème with cocoa powder, top with a dollop of vanilla whipped cream and a sprinkle of chopped candied ginger, if using.

NOTE: To make this recipe eggless, add ½ tsp of agar agar powder to the milk/tea/spice mixture and simmer for 3 minutes. Cover and steep for 10 minutes and then strain the mixture into a bowl. Whisk in the melted chocolate. Pour the mixture into the ramekins and refrigerate overnight, or until set.

DAULAT KI CHAAT CREAM PUFFS

Daulat ki Chaat is a dessert that is made with fluffy, light whipped cream flavored with saffron and cardamom. It's sold on the streets of New Delhi during the winter months. It's made by chilling fatty milk overnight in the cold air and then churning the cream for hours to get a super light, airy texture that just melts in your mouth. It's hard to re-create the same texture without putting in hours of work, but I think these cream puffs are pretty close!

MAKES
1½ DOZEN CREAM PUFFS

WHIPPED CREAM

1 tbsp (15 ml) milk

½ tsp saffron

1½ cups (360 ml) heavy whipping cream

¼ cup (30 g) powdered sugar, plus more for dusting

1 tsp vanilla extract

CHOUX PASTRY

½ cup (120 ml) water

¼ cup (54 g) butter

1 tsp granulated sugar

⅓ cup (54 g) all-purpose flour

2 eggs, plus 1 egg for wash

3 tbsp (20 g) slivered almonds

To make the whipped cream, warm the milk in a small saucepan or a microwave until it is lukewarm, about 10 seconds. Add the saffron, stir and set aside. Fit a stand mixer with a whisk attachment. Add the heavy cream and powdered sugar to the mixing bowl, and whisk on high for 4 to 5 minutes until it forms stiff peaks. Spoon half of the whipped cream into a small bowl and gently fold in the saffron milk. In the other bowl, fold in the vanilla. Place in the fridge until ready to serve.

Preheat the oven to 425°F (218°C). Line a baking sheet with parchment paper. To make the choux pastry, add the water, butter and granulated sugar to a small heavy-bottomed saucepan over medium heat. Once the mixture comes to a boil, add the flour and stir with a spatula. Keep stirring until there is a thin coating of dough on the bottom and sides of the saucepan, about 1 minute. Spoon the dough into a large bowl. Stir with a spatula for 3 to 4 minutes to help cool down the mixture. Add the 2 eggs, one at a time, mixing well in between each addition. It might look like it's curdled, but keep mixing; it will eventually come together.

Spoon the dough into a piping bag or a gallon freezer bag and snip off a 1-inch (2.5-cm) opening. Holding the piping bag directly above the parchment-lined baking sheet (at a 90-degree angle), pipe out 2-inch (5-cm) circles. If you have any points or divots in the dough, use a wet finger to smooth them out. In a small bowl, beat the remaining egg. Brush each choux pastry with the beaten egg wash. Using a spray bottle, mist the baking sheet with water once or twice. Alternatively, you can dip your hand in a little water and flick droplets onto the baking sheet.

Bake at 425°F (218°C) for 12 minutes, then reduce the temperature to 375°F (191°C) and bake for an additional 15 minutes, or until the choux pastry is golden brown. Do not open the oven door while they bake; you want the heat to dry out the center of the choux pastry. Once baked, use a toothpick or small knife to poke a hole on the side of each choux pastry and cool completely.

When ready to assemble, fold the saffron and vanilla whipped cream together so you have a streaky mixture. Fill a piping bag or freezer bag fitted with a star tip with the whipped cream. Use a serrated knife to cut the top off each choux pastry and pipe the bottom halves with whipped cream and top with a sprinkle of slivered almonds. Place the other half on top and dust with additional powdered sugar. Serve immediately or store in the fridge until ready to serve.

CARAMEL CUSTARD

Caramel custard is one of many desserts that was brought over to India during colonization. It was initially only found at ritzy, upper-crust country clubs and restaurants, but now the dessert has found its way into the home of many Indians. This recipe is a mash-up of a traditional caramel custard and a dish called lagan nu custard (wedding custard) which is served at Parsi weddings. Unlike caramel custard, lagan nu custard is spiced with cardamom and nutmeg and baked until the top has browned. This recipe has the texture of a caramel custard with the flavors of lagan nu custard.

MAKES
4 (6-OUNCE [170-G]) RAMEKINS

CARAMEL
½ cup plus 1 tbsp (115 g) granulated sugar

¼ cup (60 ml) water

CUSTARD
2 cups (480 ml) whole milk

1½ tbsp (14 g) jaggery powder (see Note)

½ tsp ground cardamom

Pinch of nutmeg

3 eggs

1 tbsp (15 g) granulated sugar

1 tsp vanilla extract

Pinch of salt

To make the caramel, add the granulated sugar and water into a small heavy-bottomed saucepan over medium-high heat. Do not stir the granulated sugar water. Let the granulated sugar dissolve and come to a boil. Keep a close eye on it as the caramel can burn quickly. It should take about 6 minutes for it to turn an amber brown. Quickly pour the caramel into the bottom of four 6-ounce (170-g) ramekins. Let the caramel set and harden for 5 minutes, then grease the sides of the ramekins with butter and set aside.

Preheat the oven to 300°F (149°C). To make the custard, add the milk, jaggery, cardamom and nutmeg to a small saucepan. Scald the milk over medium-high heat until you see bubbles on the edges of the milk. Remove the milk mixture from the stove and set aside to cool slightly.

In a medium mixing bowl, add the eggs, sugar, vanilla and salt, and whisk for 1 minute. Slowly pour in the warm milk while continuously whisking. If the milk is added too quickly, the eggs will curdle. Once all of the milk has been added in, whisk for 30 seconds and then strain the mixture into each ramekin. Place the ramekins in a 9 x 13-inch (23 x 33-cm) baking pan and pour hot water into the baking pan until the water comes halfway up the sides of the ramekins. Carefully place the baking pan into the hot oven and bake for 25 to 30 minutes, or until the middle wiggles slightly when shaken.

Remove the ramekins from the water bath using tongs and cool. Chill in the fridge overnight. When you are ready to serve the caramel custard, gently run a knife along the edges of the custard, place a serving plate on top of the ramekin and flip the plate so it's underneath the ramekin. Lift the ramekin up and the caramel custard should pop right out!

NOTE: Jaggery is used as a sweetener in many of the recipes in this book. Jaggery, or palm sugar, is an unrefined sugar that is made from palm tree sap and/or sugar cane. It is typically sold in large brown bricks which would be chiseled down into small pieces to be used for cooking. Nowadays you can find powdered jaggery easily at your local Indian grocery store. The recipes in this book call for the use of jaggery powder. If you can't find jaggery powder, you can buy a block of jaggery and grate it. It has a molasses-y, earthy flavor that is hard to replicate; however, you can use dark brown sugar or muscovado sugar as a substitute.

RICE PUDDING WITH ROASTED GRAPES (KHEER)

Kheer is truly an ancient dessert. It's been in India for almost 2,000 years, and almost every cuisine has a version of rice pudding based off kheer. We usually had it at big family get-togethers, and it was always served warm; however, it can also be served cold. I like to top mine with roasted grapes. They really add a pop of brightness to this rich, creamy dessert!

MAKES
4 SERVINGS

KHEER

¾ cup (150 g) basmati rice

1 tbsp (8 g) shelled roasted unsalted pistachios

1 tbsp (9 g) raw almonds

1 tbsp (9 g) raw cashews

3 tbsp (45 g) ghee (see Note)

7 cups (1.7 L) whole milk (see Note)

¼ cup (50 g) granulated sugar

3 tbsp (45 ml) honey (see Note)

½ tsp ground cardamom

½ tsp saffron

¼ tsp salt

ROASTED GRAPES

1½ cups (200 g) grapes (red, green or black)

1 tbsp (15 ml) honey (see Note)

½ tbsp (8 ml) balsamic vinegar

Soak the rice in water for 30 minutes and drain. Set aside. Toast the pistachios, almonds and cashews in a small nonstick skillet over medium heat for 4 minutes. Pour into a bowl to cool. Once cool, coarsely chop and set aside.

In a large saucepan, melt the ghee over medium-low heat. Add the milk and bring to a boil, stirring often to make sure the milk doesn't burn or overflow. Once the milk starts to boil, add the rice. Cook over low heat for 5 minutes, stirring often to make sure the milk doesn't boil over or burn. Add the granulated sugar, honey, cardamom, saffron and salt. Stir well and cook for 8 minutes over low heat, or until the rice is soft and cooked, stirring continuously. Remove from the heat to cool. You can serve kheer warm or cold.

When you're ready to serve, preheat the oven to 400°F (204°C). In a small bowl, toss the grapes with the honey and balsamic vinegar. Spread the grapes on a baking sheet and bake for 15 minutes. Spoon about 1 cup (220 g) of kheer into 4 bowls. Top with the roasted grapes and chopped nuts.

NOTE: You can make this dessert vegan by using your choice of non-dairy milk, maple syrup instead of honey and vegan margarine or butter instead of ghee.

BERRY BHAPA DOI

Bhapa doi is a Bengali dessert made with yogurt and jaggery. This simple, baked yogurt dessert is silky smooth and, I would like to think, healthy-ish. The texture reminds me of panna cotta, but without all of the fuss! Most of the sweetness comes from the berries, so feel free to play with the amount of sweetened condensed milk so that the sweetness level is to your liking.

MAKES
4 (4-OUNCE [113-G]) RAMEKINS

½ cup (120 ml) heavy whipping cream (see Note)

½ cup (47 g) fresh raspberries

1 tbsp (20 g) blueberries, about 10 berries

3 strawberries, destemmed

1 cup (160 g) plain Greek yogurt (see Note)

¼ cup (60 ml) sweetened condensed milk (see Note)

1 tsp vanilla extract

½ cup (113 g) fresh berries, for garnish

Preheat the oven to 215°F (102°C).

Add the heavy cream and berries to a blender, and blend until smooth, about 20 seconds. Strain the mixture into a mixing bowl. Add the yogurt, sweetened condensed milk and vanilla. Whisk well.

Divide the yogurt mixture into the ramekins. Place the ramekins in a 9 x 13-inch (23 x 33-cm) baking pan and fill the pan with water until it comes halfway up the sides of the ramekins. Cover with foil and bake for 25 to 30 minutes, or until the center is barely set and wiggles a little when gently shaken. Cool and chill the bhapa doi in the refrigerator for at least 4 hours. Top with additional berries when ready to serve.

NOTE: Feel free to change up the fruit and use whatever is seasonal and local to you! You can also use coconut cream, coconut yogurt or sweetened condensed coconut milk to make this dish vegan.

TOASTED SESAME CRÈME BRÛLÉE

Nutty, with a sugar-y crunch, this crème brûlée has it all! This recipe is inspired by til chikki, a sesame seed brittle. My mom would put them in my lunchbox as a treat when I was growing up. I was always eyeing the other kids' desserts, so I'd often trade my til chikki in for a processed candy bar. Now that I'm older, I wouldn't trade them for anything! The best part about this recipe is that while the crème brûlée bakes, the sesame seeds rise to the top so when you make the sugar crust, you get a thin til chikki.

MAKES
4 (6-OUNCE [170-G]) RAMEKINS

1 tbsp (7 g) white sesame seeds

1½ cups (360 ml) heavy cream

¾ cup (180 ml) whole milk

1 tsp roasted sesame paste (see Note)

1 tsp vanilla extract

8 egg yolks

⅔ plus ¼ cup (182 g) granulated sugar, divided

¼ tsp salt

Preheat the oven to 325°F (163°C). Place ramekins in a roasting pan.

Add the sesame seeds to a small nonstick skillet over medium heat. Toast for 3 to 4 minutes, or until they turn golden brown. Pour the sesame seeds into a sandwich bag and crush the seeds with a rolling pin by rolling over the bag with pressure 6 to 8 times.

Pour the sesame seeds, heavy cream, milk, roasted sesame paste and vanilla into a small saucepan. Scald the milk over medium heat while stirring, making sure the sesame paste is completely dissolved. After about 2 minutes, bubbles should start forming around the edges of the pan. Remove the mixture from the heat and set aside.

In a separate bowl, whisk the egg yolks, ⅔ cup (128 g) of granulated sugar and salt for 1 minute. Slowly pour the hot milk mixture into the egg mixture while continuously stirring to make sure the eggs don't curdle. Mix for 1 minute. Evenly divide the mixture into the ramekins. Pour hot water into the roasting pan until the water reaches half way up the sides of the ramekins. Cover the pan with foil and carefully place the pan into the oven. Bake for 25 to 30 minutes, or until the middle of the crème brûlée has just set. Remove the ramekins from the pan and let cool for 4 to 5 hours at room temperature.

When ready to serve, sprinkle an even layer of the remaning ¼ cup (50 g) of granulated sugar onto each crème brûlée and use a blowtorch to melt the granulated sugar until it caramelizes. If you don't have a torch, you can place the crème brûlée under the broiler for a couple seconds, making sure to keep a close eye on it.

 NOTE: You can find roasted sesame paste at any Asian grocery store like 99 Ranch or H-Mart, or online.

CARROT CAKE PUDDING (GAJAR NO HALWO)

Gajar no halwo is a pudding made by cooking down grated carrots in milk and ghee. It is sweetened with sugar and spiced with a hint of cardamom. It always reminded me of carrot cake, and I figured why not mash the two together! You can make this recipe vegan by using your choice of non-dairy milk and vegan butter instead of ghee.

MAKES
2 TO 4 SERVINGS

3 tbsp (33 g) raw chopped walnuts

1 tbsp (15 g) ghee

2 cups (220 g) carrots, grated

1 cup (240 ml) milk

⅓ cup (66 g) granulated sugar

2 tbsp (28 g) dark brown sugar

½ tsp ground cinnamon

¼ tsp ground ginger

¼ tsp ground nutmeg

¼ tsp salt

1 tbsp (10 g) raisins

Add the walnuts to a small nonstick skillet over medium heat. Toast for 4 minutes and pour into a bowl to cool. In a large nonstick saucepan, add the ghee and melt over medium heat. Add the grated carrots and sauté for 5 minutes.

Pour in the milk and cook for 5 minutes, stirring occasionally. Add the granulated sugar, brown sugar, cinnamon, ginger, nutmeg and salt and mix well. Cook for another 8 minutes, or until most of the liquid has evaporated and the carrots are tender. Mix in the walnuts and raisins. Serve the gajar no halwo warm or room temperature. You can garnish it with additional walnuts before serving.

 NOTE: You can use the same method to make beet or bottle gourd (doodhi) halwo; just substitute the carrots with grated beets or bottle gourd squash.

HOT CHOCOLATE KULFI

When I was younger my grandma would bring me a Fudgsicle when she would pick me up from school during the summer. We'd walk home hand in hand enjoying our frozen treats. When she got older, she moved to India and whenever I would visit her, she would give me money to sneak away and pick up an ice cream for us from the corner store. Our little secret inspired this kulfi recipe, which uses the traditional method of boiling full-fat milk down until it is thick and creamy.

MAKES
6 TO 10 SERVINGS, DEPENDING ON THE SIZE OF THE MOLD

4 cups (960 ml) whole milk

¾ cup (180 ml) heavy cream

⅔ cup (115 g) high-quality milk chocolate morsels

¼ tsp salt

½ tsp ground cinnamon

¼ cup (40 g) roasted unsalted almonds, finely chopped

Add the milk, heavy cream, chocolate, salt and cinnamon into a heavy-bottom saucepan over medium-high heat. Stir continuously until the milk comes to a boil, about 6 minutes. Simmer on low heat for 30 minutes, stirring often. Make sure to keep an eye on the milk as it might overflow. Add the chopped almonds and simmer for an additional 5 minutes. The mixture should be thick enough to coat the back of a spoon. Pour the mixture into ice pop molds and freeze for at least 5 hours. Set the kulfi out on the counter for 5 minutes before unmolding.

 NOTE: To make a no-mess, no-drip version for your kids, use a block of Abuelita Mexican chocolate instead of regular chocolate. It contains carrageenan, a thickener made from seaweed, which prevents the kulfi from dripping all over the place!

ETON MESS WITH RHUBARB-ROSE COMPOTE AND COCONUT CREAM

This is one of those desserts that tastes like it took forever to make, but in reality, it's just whipped cream, fruit compote and crushed meringues all carelessly spooned into a bowl. It's a medley of textures and flavors; crunchy and sweet meringue offset by floral and tart rhubarb-rose compote all topped with a light coconut whipped cream. All the flavors meld together beautifully and perfectly balance each other.

MAKES
4 TO 6 SERVINGS

COCONUT WHIPPED CREAM
1 (14-oz [396-g]) can coconut cream or full-fat coconut milk

1 tbsp (8 g) powdered sugar

MERINGUES
2 egg whites

¼ tsp cream of tartar

⅔ cup (132 g) granulated sugar

1 tsp vanilla extract

RHUBARB-ROSE COMPOTE
3½ cups (385 g) rhubarb (about 3 stalks), ¼-inch (6-mm)-thick slices

7 tbsp (85 g) granulated sugar

¼ tsp salt

1 tsp rose water

1¼ cups (206 g) raspberries, for serving

1½ cups (216 g) strawberries, halved, for serving

Place the can of coconut cream in the fridge overnight.

Preheat the oven to 215°F (102°C). Line a baking sheet with parchment paper and fit a stand mixer with the whisk attachment.

To make the meringues, add the egg whites to the bowl of the stand mixer and whisk on medium-low. When the egg whites are foamy, add the cream of tartar. Whisk for 30 seconds. Increase the mixer speed to medium and slowly add the granulated sugar to the egg whites. Once all of the granulated sugar has been added, add the vanilla. Turn up the mixer to its highest setting and mix for 10 minutes. Test the meringue by taking a little bit and rubbing it between two fingers. If you can feel the granulated sugar crystals, continue whisking on high. Test again and keep whisking until the meringue is completely smooth.

Spoon about ½ cup (110 g) of the meringue onto the parchment-lined baking sheet and spread into a 3-inch (7-cm) disc. Repeat until all of the meringue is on the baking tray. Bake for 20 to 30 minutes, or until the meringues easily lift off the parchment paper. Turn off the oven, leaving the meringues in the oven. Remove the meringues when the oven has cooled, about an hour.

To make the rhubarb-rose compote, add the rhubarb slices, granulated sugar and salt into a saucepan over medium-low heat. Cook for 15 minutes, stirring often. Remove from the heat and stir in the rose water. Pour into a jar and let cool completely.

Make the coconut whipped cream. If using full-fat coconut milk, open the can and drain away any of the liquid. Add the coconut cream to a bowl with the powdered sugar. Whisk well until you have a light, airy whipped cream. Place a dollop of the whipped cream into each serving bowl. Top with crushed meringues, rhubarb rose compote and fresh berries.

NOTE: Don't worry about plating it perfectly, it's an abstract painting, not a precise masterpiece! This is also a great dessert to make-ahead for a party! You can set up a little eton mess bar and let your guests plate their own dessert!

MATCHA TAPIOCA PUDDING (SABUDHANA NI KHEER)

Tapioca pudding is a dish that is familiar to people all over the world. Every country seems to have their own version. Sabudhana ni kheer is a pudding made with tapioca pearls (sabudhana) and milk. It is typically spiced with saffron and cardamom and topped with various chopped nuts. This version is made with matcha, a Japanese green tea powder, and a hint of cinnamon! The earthiness and mellow flavor of the matcha really lends itself to this comforting pudding.

MAKES
2 TO 4 SERVINGS

⅓ cup (83 g) small tapioca pearls (sabudhana)

3 cups (720 ml) coconut milk

4-inch (10-cm) piece cinnamon stick

4 tsp (8 g) matcha powder

¼ cup (50 g) granulated sugar, or to taste

Unsweetened shredded coconut, for garnish, optional

Soak the tapioca pearls in water for 30 minutes. Add the coconut milk, drained tapioca pearls and cinnamon stick to a medium saucepan over medium heat.

In a small bowl, mix together the matcha powder and 4 tablespoons (60 ml) of hot water until smooth. Add the matcha paste into the saucepan with the coconut milk and whisk well. Add the sugar and bring the milk to a boil over medium heat, and then simmer over low heat for 20 minutes or until the tapioca pearls are cooked. Garnish with shredded coconut, if using, and serve the pudding warm or cold.

SMALL BITES

There is a saying in Gujarati, "muh mithu karo," which means "sweeten your mouth." It's usually said as an exclamation after someone has had something good happen to them. Whether it be a new job or your favorite sports team winning a championship, Indians will find any excuse to hit up the local mithaiwala (sweet shop)!

The recipes from this chapter are inspired by some of my favorite mithai. Mithai is a general term for Indian desserts and sweets. Most of the mithai from this chapter fall into the burfi, ladva/laddoo or milk fudge category. Milk fudges are made with milk solids and condensed milk, while ladva/laddoo are toasted flour or nut-based sweets that are rolled into balls. Burfi can be made from either milk, flour or nuts, and are cut into bite-size squares. These mithai are usually bought at specialty shops and given out during holidays and special life events. Also, since these desserts are very rich, they are usually presented as small bites.

Some of the recipes that are in this chapter are traditional, like Besan Burfi (a toasted chickpea flour fudge, page 58) and some of the recipes are more modern, like my Guava Pâté de Fruits (page 53) and Jaggery Caramel Peanut Clusters (page 61). But all of the recipes have one thing in common: they're small bites meant to sweeten your mouth and to remind you to savor the sweet moments that happen in your life.

DULCE DE LECHE PENDA

Penda, or peda, was the most popular mithai in my household. It's a fudge made with khoya, which is made by cooking down whole milk until all of the liquid has evaporated and you're left with just the solid milk fat. It's pretty time consuming, so I used a well-known shortcut and used nonfat dry milk powder and sweetened condensed milk. I toasted the milk powder and used dulce de leche to pump up the caramel flavor! Feel free to use store-bought dulce de leche to shorten the cook time.

MAKES
10 PENDA

DULCE DE LECHE
1 (14-oz [396-g]) can sweetened condensed milk

PENDA
½ cup (46 g) instant nonfat dry milk powder

⅓ cup (100 g) dulce de leche

1 tbsp (15 g) ghee

1 tbsp (15 ml) whole milk

¼ tsp ground cinnamon

¼ tsp salt

¼ cup (45 g) dark chocolate chips

½ tsp coconut oil

Flaky sea salt

To make the dulce de leche, remove the paper wrapper on the can of sweetened condensed milk and place the can in a saucepan. Cover the can with enough water so that the can is completely submerged under water. Place the saucepan on the stove over medium heat and bring the water to a boil, then turn the heat down and simmer for 3 hours. Keep a close eye on the pan, as you might need to top off the pan with more water as it evaporates. When done, remove the can and let cool completely.

To make the penda, start by preheating the oven to 300°F (149°C) and line a baking sheet with parchment paper. Spread the milk powder in a thin layer on the parchment-lined baking sheet. Bake for 9 to 10 minutes, or until the powder is golden brown.

Pour the toasted milk powder into a nonstick pan with the dulce de leche over medium-low heat. Stir for 3 minutes. Add the ghee, milk, cinnamon and salt and mix well. Continuously stir the mixture for 5 minutes, or until the mixture thickens and starts leaving the sides of the pan. Remove the pan from the heat and cool for 5 minutes.

Grease your hands with ghee and roll 1 tablespoon (15 g) of the dough into a ball. Repeat with the rest of the dough. Gently flatten the balls with your hands and use your pointer finger to create a little divot in the middle of each penda.

Set up a bain-marie by bringing a small pot of water to a boil and placing a small bowl on top of the pot, making sure the bowl does not touch the water. Add the chocolate and coconut oil to the bowl and stir until melted, about 2 minutes. You can also add the coconut oil and chocolate to a microwave-safe bowl and microwave until the chocolate is melted, about 1 minute. Mix well and pour the chocolate into a small sandwich bag. Snip off the end and pipe the chocolate into the divots in each penda. Top with a sprinkle of the flaky sea salt. Let the penda set for at least 3 hours. The texture will become less chewy as they set over time. Store in an airtight container for up to 2 weeks.

DATE AND NUT TRUFFLES (KHAJUR PAK)

This is a play on khajur pak, a date and nut roll that is sliced into small pieces. It's sugar-free, vegan and comes together in no time. It's a great healthy sweet treat for lunchboxes or a way to satisfy your sweet tooth without the guilt!

MAKES
20 TRUFFLES

12 Medjool dates, pitted

¼ cup (36 g) raw almonds

¼ cup (36 g) raw cashews

¼ cup (30 g) shelled raw pistachios

1 tsp flaxseed meal

1 tsp amaranth seeds, optional

½ tsp ground cinnamon

Pinch of salt

¼ cup (20 g) finely shredded unsweetened coconut

Soak the dates in hot water for 10 minutes. While the dates are soaking, toast the nuts by adding the almonds, cashews and pistachios to a small nonstick skillet over medium-high heat. Stir continuously for 4 to 5 minutes then add to a food processor.

Drain the dates and put them in the food processor with the toasted nuts, flaxseed meal, amaranth seeds (if using), cinnamon and salt. Pulse 5 to 8 times until the dates and nuts have turned into a sticky, chunky mixture. Spoon the date mixture into a bowl and mix well with a spatula. Let cool.

While the date mixture cools, toast the coconut in a small nonstick skillet, stirring often, over medium heat until nice and golden brown, about 3 minutes. Pour the toasted coconut into a bowl and cool.

Take 1 tablespoon (25 g) of the date mixture and roll it into a ball in between your hands. Repeat with the rest of the date mixture. Roll each date and nut truffle in the toasted coconut until it's completely coated. Place the truffles on a dish and refrigerate for 15 minutes to set. Serve immediately or store in an airtight container in the fridge for up to 1 week.

COCONUT BURFI CHOCOLATE BARK

Growing up, coconut burfi always reminded me of the filling in Mounds bars. Intensely coconut-y and sweet! I decided to lean into it and made this simple coconut burfi bark. This bark has a soft cardamom-coconut filling sandwiched between two thin layers of dark chocolate.

MAKES
3 DOZEN

2 cups (326 g) dark chocolate morsels (see Note)

2 cups (205 g) finely shredded unsweetened coconut

1 tsp cardamom seeds, finely crushed

½ tsp salt

⅔ cup (160 ml) sweetened condensed milk

Line a 9 x 9-inch (23 x 23-cm) pan with parchment paper.

Add the chocolate to a microwavable bowl, and microwave in 15-second increments, stirring between each increment, until all of the chocolate is melted. Alternatively, if you don't have a microwave, set up a bain-marie by bringing a small pot of water to a boil and placing a small bowl on top of the pot, making sure the bowl does not touch the water. Add the chocolate to the bowl and stir until melted, about 5 minutes.

Pour half of the chocolate on the parchment-lined baking pan and spread evenly. Place into the freezer to set for 15 minutes, or until set. While the chocolate sets, add the coconut, cardamom and salt to a small saucepan. Stir over medium heat for 1 minute. Pour the coconut mixture into a medium mixing bowl and add the sweetened condensed milk. Mix until well combined.

Remove the pan from the freezer and evenly spread the coconut burfi mixture over the chocolate. Pour the rest of the melted chocolate on top and spread evenly. Place the pan back in the freezer for 15 more minutes, or until set. Cut the bark into small bite-size pieces, 1½-inch (4-cm) squares. Store in an airtight container in the fridge for up to 2 weeks.

NOTE: I suggest using melting chocolate or almond bark (you can find these in the baking aisle in your grocery store) since they are easier to work with and set faster.

CASHEW FUDGE BARS (KAJU KATLI)

I went through a phase where I was addicted to kaju katli. I could easily house a whole tray of them, no problem! The texture is like a dense fudge and the silver leaf (vark) on top makes them so eye-catching. Also, this dessert is gluten-free and can be made vegan!

MAKES
1 (9 X 9-INCH [23 X 23-CM]) PAN, ABOUT 54 PIECES

1 tsp ghee or vegan butter, for greasing

4¾ cups (696 g) cashews

1½ cups (300 g) granulated sugar

⅔ cup plus 1 tablespoon (155 ml) water

½ tsp ground cardamom

¼ tsp salt

Silver or gold leaf, optional

Grease a large dinner plate and a 9 x 9-inch (23 x 23-cm) pan with ghee.

Add the cashews to a blender and process until you have a very fine powder, about 1 minute. Set aside.

In a medium nonstick pan, add the granulated sugar and water. Bring the granulated sugar and water to a boil over medium heat. Once the syrup comes to a boil, continue cooking for 2 minutes or until the sugar syrup reaches one-string consistency. You can check for one-string consistency by dipping a spoon into the syrup, letting it cool for a few seconds, and taking a very tiny amount of the syrup, rubbing it between your thumb and pointer finger and gently pulling them apart. If you see a single string is formed and it does not break when your pointer finger and your thumb are pulled apart, then the syrup is done.

Add the cashew powder, cardamom and salt to the sugar water. Mix well and cook over low heat for 3 minutes while stirring continuously so that the mixture thickens. Spoon the mixture onto the greased plate and let cool for 5 minutes. Grease your hands with ghee and knead the mixture for 3 to 4 minutes; if the mixture feels too hot, let it cool for a couple more minutes. Evenly press the dough into the greased pan. Cool completely and cut into 1 x 1½-inch (2.5 x 4-cm) size pieces. If you want to make them look extra fancy, press silver or gold leaf onto the top of each kaju katli. Store in an airtight container for up to 1 week.

NOTE: Be sure to blend the cashews down so that the powder is as fine as you can get it without making cashew butter. The finer the cashew powder, the smoother the cashew fudge will be.

ALMOND CARDAMOM BRITTLE (ALMOND CHIKKI)

Chikki is any brittle made with jaggery powder and sugar. What I've learned is that there is good chikki and bad chikki. Bad chikki sticks to your teeth and is as hard as a rock. Good chikki just falls apart and almost melts in your mouth. This recipe is for good chikki. The baking soda gives it an airy texture so it's crunchy, but won't break your teeth, and still has that traditional jaggery flavor!

MAKES
ABOUT 24 PIECES

1¼ cups (179 g) raw almonds

⅔ cup (96 g) jaggery powder

¼ cup (60 ml) light corn syrup

1 tbsp (15 g) ghee, divided

1 tbsp (15 ml) water

½ tsp cardamom seeds, finely crushed

1 tsp baking soda

¼ tsp fine salt

Flaky sea salt

Line a 9 x 13–inch (23 x 33–cm) baking sheet with parchment paper and grease with cooking spray.

Add the almonds to a nonstick skillet over medium-low heat. Toast the almonds for 5 minutes, stirring continuously. When done, coarsely chop the almonds and set aside.

In a medium nonstick saucepan, add the jaggery powder, corn syrup, ½ tablespoon (7 g) of ghee, water and cardamom. Bring to a boil over medium-low heat until it reaches 300°F (149°C), about 10 minutes. If you don't have a thermometer, drop a small amount of the brittle into a glass of cold water. If the brittle hardens into threads that are easily broken once cooled, it's ready. Add the chopped almonds, baking soda, fine salt and ½ tablespoon (7 g) of ghee. Remove from the heat and mix well.

Pour the mixture onto the greased parchment-lined baking sheet. Use a spatula to press the chikki until it is ¼ inch (6 mm) thick. You can also place another sheet of greased parchment paper on top and use a rolling pin to flatten the chikki. Sprinkle some flaky sea salt on top and press the salt in with a spatula. Let it cool completely and break into small pieces. Store in an airtight container for up to 1 month.

GUAVA PÂTÉ DE FRUITS

When I initially started doing research for this cookbook, I came across Bombay Karachi halwa, a translucent, orange-hued saffron halwa made from cornstarch, similar to Turkish delights. They inspired me to make these gorgeous guava pâté de fruits, or gummy candies. They look like little jewels and are a great gift to impress your friends with!

MAKES
ABOUT 81 PIECES

2 cups (480 ml) 100% guava juice

1 tbsp (15 ml) fresh lemon juice

1½ cups (300 g) granulated sugar, divided

¾ cup (180 ml) liquid pectin

Line a 9 x 9-inch (23 x 23-cm) pan with parchment paper and lightly spray with cooking spray.

Add the guava juice, lemon juice and ½ cup (100 g) of granulated sugar to a large saucepan over medium-high heat. Continuously stir the mixture until it reaches 140°F (60°C), about 10 minutes, and add in the liquid pectin and ½ cup (100 g) of sugar. Lower the heat to medium and keep stirring the mixture. When the mixture hits 200°F (93°C), which should take about 10 minutes, lower the heat so that it holds at 200°F (93°C) for 3 minutes and keep stirring. Turn the heat up back to medium and keep stirring and until it hits 230°F (110°C), which should take about 5 minutes. Lower the heat again to hold the temperature at 235°F (113°C) for 3 minutes.

Pour the guava mixture into the prepared baking pan. Allow to cool to room temperature and set for at least 12 hours. Do not put the pâté de fruits in the fridge. The humidity in the fridge will make the pâté de fruits soft and gooey. Once the pâté de fruits is set, cut the slab into small 1-inch (2.5-cm) square pieces. Gently coat the pâté de fruits in the remaining ½ cup (100 g) of sugar and place in a sealed container until ready to serve.

PEANUT LADDOO BUCKEYE BALLS

I re-created an American classic using peanut laddoos, a peanut and jaggery mixture that is blended and rolled into small bite-size balls. These peanut laddoos have a gritty, Butterfinger-esque texture that will blow your mind. These are great to pop into your kid's lunchboxes for a sweet treat. If you're feeling particularly lazy (hey, it happens to all of us!), feel free to skip the chocolate coating and enjoy them on their own!

MAKES
17 BALLS

1 cup (150 g) roasted unsalted peanuts

⅔ cup (96 g) jaggery powder

2 tbsp (30 g) ghee, plus more for greasing

¼ tsp cardamom seeds, finely crushed

¼ tsp kosher salt

¾ cup (122 g) milk chocolate morsels

1 tsp coconut oil

Add the peanuts to a small skillet over medium heat. Toast for 3 minutes, stirring continuously. Add the peanuts to a food processer and process until it is a fine powder. Add the jaggery, ghee, cardamom and salt and process for 2 to 3 minutes, scraping down the sides every so often. The mixture should easily form a ball if you squeeze it with your fist.

Pour the mixture into a medium bowl and grease your hands with ghee. Tightly pack a tablespoon (14 g) with the peanut mixture. Give the peanut laddoo mixture a squeeze with your fist and then gently roll the dough into a ball. If your peanut mixture is too crumbly, add an additional tablespoon (15 g) of ghee and mix well and try rolling again. Place all of the laddoos onto a plate and freeze for 1 hour.

Add the milk chocolate morsels and coconut oil to a microwavable bowl, and microwave in 15-second increments, stirring between each increment until all of the chocolate is melted, about 1 to 2 minutes. Alternatively, if you don't have a microwave, set up a bain-marie by bringing a small pot of water to a boil and placing a small bowl on top of the pot, making sure the bowl does not touch the water. Add the chocolate and coconut oil to the bowl and stir until melted, about 2 to 3 minutes. Remove the chocolate from the heat.

Line a baking sheet with parchment paper. Insert a toothpick into a peanut laddoo and dip it into the chocolate. Place the ball onto the parchment-lined baking sheet and remove the toothpick. If it's stuck, use another toothpick to push the laddoo off the inserted toothpick. Coat the rest of the laddoos with chocolate. Place in the freezer for 10 minutes or until the chocolate is set. Gently use your finger to smooth off the peanut laddoo to cover the toothpick holes. Store in an airtight container in the fridge for up to 2 weeks.

BANANA COCONUT BURFI

Soft, gooey banana fudge with chopped walnuts to give it texture. This mithai reminds me of banana bread batter.

MAKES
36 BALLS

½ cup (60 g) raw walnuts, chopped

4 bananas

½ cup (120 ml) milk

¼ cup (60 ml) sweetened condensed milk

1 cup (90 g) finely shredded unsweetened coconut

¼ tsp ground cinnamon

¼ cup (50 g) granulated sugar, or to taste

¼ tsp kosher salt

½ cup (56 g) cocoa powder or finely shredded coconut, for dusting

Toast the chopped walnuts in a small skillet over medium heat for 5 minutes. Be sure to stir continuously so the walnuts don't burn. Pour the walnuts into a small bowl to cool. Once cooled, chop into smaller pieces.

Add the bananas to a blender and purée until smooth. If you don't have a blender, just add the bananas to a bowl and use a fork to mash them. Add the milk to a medium saucepan over medium-low heat. Bring the milk to a boil, stirring occasionally. Then add the banana purée and stir well. Cook for 15 minutes, stirring continuously. Add the sweetened condensed milk, coconut, cinnamon, granulated sugar and salt. Mix well. Cook for an additional 10 minutes. Fold in the walnuts and cook for another 8 to 10 minutes. Most of the liquid should be evaporated so you have a mixture that is easily moldable. Cook the mixture until you can press a spatula into the mixture and leave a dent. Spoon the mixture into a bowl and cool completely. Refrigerate the mixture for 4 hours or overnight.

Pour the cocoa powder into a bowl. Lightly wet your hands with cold water and take 1 tablespoon (15 g) of the banana coconut burfi mixture and roll it into a ball. Roll the banana coconut burfi in the cocoa powder until covered and place on a plate. Repeat until all of the mixture is done. Place the plate of burfi in the fridge to set for at least 4 hours; overnight is best. Store the truffles in the fridge for up to 4 days.

NOTE: You can also freeze the burfi balls for up to 1 month. They will have a similar texture to banana "nice" cream!

BESAN BURFI (CHICKPEA FLOUR FUDGE)

Every state in India has a dessert that they are famous for, and in Gujarat, it's besan burfi, also known as magaz. The main flavor comes from toasting fine chickpea flour until it has a nutty fragrance and then mixing it with powdered sugar to sweeten it. The burfi has a super smooth consistency that just melts in your mouth!

MAKES
18 BURFIS

1½ cups (330 g) ghee, plus more for greasing

3 cups (390 g) chickpea flour

3 tbsp (30 g) semolina

1½ cups (180 g) powdered sugar

1½ tsp (3 g) cardamom powder

¼ tsp salt

3 tbsp (20 g) sliced almonds

Generously grease a 9 x 5-inch (23 x 13-cm) loaf pan with ½ tablespoon (7 g) of ghee and set aside.

Heat the ghee in a medium saucepan over low heat. Once the ghee melts, add the chickpea flour and semolina. Cook while stirring continuously for 10 to 12 minutes. The chickpea flour will start to change colors to a darker yellow/brown and start smelling nutty. Pour the mixture into a medium bowl. Add the powdered sugar, cardamom and salt. Mix well and be careful not to touch the burfi mixture; it's very hot!

Pour the mixture into the greased loaf pan and smooth out. Tap the pan on the counter a couple of times to get rid of any air bubbles. Sprinkle with the sliced almonds and place it in the fridge overnight to set. Once the besan burfi has set, cut into 1½-inch (4-cm) squares. Store in an airtight container in the fridge for up to 2 weeks.

JAGGERY CARAMEL PEANUT CLUSTERS

A modern take on mithai, these clusters feature roasted peanuts mixed with buttery jaggery caramel and dipped in chocolate.

MAKES
16 CLUSTERS

¼ cup (60 ml) light corn syrup

½ cup (100 g) granulated sugar

½ cup (72 g) jaggery powder

¾ cup (180 ml) heavy cream

¼ cup (57 g) unsalted butter, softened

1¼ cups (200 g) roasted unsalted peanuts

½ tsp kosher salt

¾ cup (203 g) milk chocolate morsels or almond bark

1 tbsp (15 g) flaky sea salt

Line a baking sheet with parchment paper.

In a heavy-bottomed saucepan over medium heat, add the corn syrup, granulated sugar and jaggery. Cook until the sugars dissolve, about 5 minutes. Add the heavy cream and butter and mix well. Cook over medium heat until the caramel is 250°F (121°C), about 20 minutes. Take off the heat and stir in the peanuts and salt. Let the peanut caramel cool for 8 minutes. Create 2-tablespoon (30-g) dollops of the peanut caramel and drop onto the parchment-lined baking sheet. Place each dollop about 2 inches (5 cm) apart. Let the caramel cool completely.

Add the milk chocolate morsels into a microwavable bowl, and microwave in 15-second increments, stirring between each increment, until all of the chocolate is melted, about 2 minutes. Alternatively, if you don't have a microwave, set up a bain-marie by bringing a small pot of water to a boil and placing a small bowl on top of the pot, making sure the bowl does not touch the water. Add the chocolate to the bowl and stir until melted, about 3 minutes. Remove the chocolate from the heat.

Use a fork to dip each peanut cluster into the melted chocolate and tap off the excess chocolate. Place each chocolate-coated candy back onto the parchment sheet and sprinkle with flaky sea salt. Once all of the caramel peanut clusters are coated in chocolate, place the baking tray in the fridge for 15 minutes or until the chocolate is set. Store in an airtight container at room temperature for up to 2 weeks.

RAVA NA LADVA

Rava na ladva is a traditional sweet made with toasted semolina (rava) and durum wheat flour mixed with ghee and nuts rolled into small balls. They are usually served during festivals and are very simple to make. My version is mildly sweet. Be sure to taste the mixture before rolling out to make sure the sweetness is to your liking.

MAKES
12 BALLS

¼ cup (36 g) raw cashews

2 tbsp (30 g) ghee, plus more for your hands

1 tbsp (13 g) raisins

1 cup (185 g) semolina

¼ cup (32 g) durum wheat flour or whole wheat flour

¼ cup (27 g) finely shredded unsweetened coconut

½ cup (51 g) almond meal or ground almonds

¼ cup (36 g) jaggery powder

¼ cup (50 g) granulated sugar, or to taste

¼ tsp salt

½ cup (120 ml) whole milk

Coarsely chop the cashews and set aside.

In a medium skillet over medium heat, melt the ghee. Add the chopped cashews and raisins and cook for 30 seconds while stirring continuously. Add the semolina and durum wheat flour and cook for 5 minutes, while stirring continuously so that the semolina doesn't burn. Add the shredded coconut and almond meal, and stir for an additional 2 minutes. Add the jaggery, granulated sugar and salt and stir for 1 minute. The mixture should look like light brown wet sand at this point.

Pour the mixture into a medium bowl and let the mixture cool for 5 minutes. Add the milk a tablespoon (15 ml) at a time, mixing well in between each addition. Grease your hands with a teaspoon of ghee and take 2 tightly packed tablespoons (40 g) of the mixture and press tightly into a ball with your fist. Keep pressing and gently rolling until you have a round ball/laddoo. If the mixture is too crumbly, add an additional tablespoon (15 ml) of milk, mix well and try again. Roll out all of your ladva. Store in an airtight container in the fridge for up to 1 week.

NOTE: Be sure to measure out the ingredients before getting started as the semolina burns easily and you have to move quickly!

WHOLE WHEAT LADVA (CHURMA NA LADVA)

Every Diwali, the Hindu new year, my mom would make big, fat churma na ladva and hide a quarter in one of them. The idea was that the person who gets the ladva with the coin is considered lucky for the upcoming new year. I got in trouble more than once for smashing all of the ladva to find the coin before anyone else could get it. I would also resort to eating way more ladva than I could handle just to get the one with the coin. Churma na ladva are made by forming dough with whole wheat flour and chickpea flour (the mixture is known as churma) and then deep frying it in ghee and lightly sweetening it with jaggery. In order to make these just a teensy bit healthier, my mom would make flatbreads out of the dough and toast them on a skillet before processing them.

MAKES
17 LADVA

½ cup (65 g) chickpea flour

2½ cups (320 g) durum wheat flour or whole wheat flour

1 cup plus 3 tbsp (285 ml) ghee, melted, divided

1 cup (240 ml) lukewarm water

¼ cup (36 g) raw unsalted almonds

2 tbsp (16 g) shelled unsalted pistachios

1 tbsp (9 g) cashews

1½ tsp (3 g) ground cardamom

1½ cups (216 g) jaggery powder

1 tbsp (7 g) white poppy seeds

Add the chickpea flour and durum wheat flour to a mixing bowl. Whisk well and add 3 tablespoons (45 ml) of the melted ghee. Use your fingers to rub the flour into the ghee for 2 minutes, or until the mixture has a sandy texture without any lumps of ghee. Add 1 cup (240 ml) of lukewarm water and mix until it comes together into a lightly wet dough. If the dough feels dry, add additional water, and if the dough feels too wet, add additional durum wheat flour 1 teaspoon at a time until you reach the texture that is needed.

Divide the dough into 7 evenly-sized balls that are about the size of a large lemon. Place a large nonstick skillet over high heat. Roll the dough balls into 6-inch (15-cm)-wide circles that are ¼ inch (6 mm) thick. Carefully place the flatbread onto the hot skillet over high heat and cook for 2½ to 3 minutes on each side, or until the edges are browned and the center is lightly toasted.

While the flatbreads cool down, toast the nuts. Add ½ teaspoon of ghee to a nonstick skillet over medium-low heat. Add the nuts and toast, stirring continuously, for 2 minutes or until lightly browned. Cool for 2 minutes and blend into a coarse powder in a food processor.

Crumble the flatbreads into bite-size pieces. Blend the mixture in a food processor or blender in two batches. Blend until it is the texture of fine sand. Pour the mixture into a large mixing bowl. Add the cardamom and nut powder mixture.

In a nonstick pan over medium-low heat, add 1 cup (240 ml) melted ghee and the jaggery. Stir continuously until all of the jaggery has dissolved into a smooth liquid. The ghee and jaggery will stay separated while it melts.

Once the jaggery has dissolved, pour the hot mixture into the flour mixture and use a spatula to mix well. Once the ladva mixture is cool enough to handle, take ¼ cup (71 g) of the mixture and use your fist to squeeze the mixture into a ball. Continue until all of the mixture is formed into ladva. Place the white poppy seeds into a bowl and roll the ladvas into the poppy seeds so that they're sparsely covered. Enjoy while warm or room temperature.

SESAME SEED BRITTLE (TIL CHIKKI)

Til chikki is a sesame seed brittle made with jaggery. I like to roll out the brittle so thin that it easily breaks apart and melts in your mouth. You can crush a few pieces of chikki over ice cream or any creamy dessert to add some crunch and nuttiness to it!

MAKES
8 TO 10 SERVINGS

¾ cup (100 g) white sesame seeds

¼ cup (33 g) black sesame seeds

1 tbsp (5 g) unsalted butter

1 cup (144 g) jaggery powder

Line a baking sheet with parchment paper and set aside. Add water and 2 to 3 cubes of ice to a small glass.

In a large nonstick pan, toast the sesame seeds over medium heat for 4 minutes, stirring often. Pour the sesame seeds in a bowl to cool. In the same pan, melt the butter. Add the jaggery powder and stir over low heat for 4 to 5 minutes.

Take a small dollop of the jaggery syrup and drop it into the glass of ice water. Wait 5 seconds and check the consistency of the sugar ball. It should be hard and should snap if broken. If the ball is still soft, cook the jaggery for another minute and test again.

Once the jaggery reaches the hard crack stage, add the sesame seeds and mix well. Spoon the mixture onto the parchment-lined baking sheet. Place another piece of parchment on top and use a rolling pin to roll the brittle out until it is ⅛ inch (3 mm) thick. Score the brittle in 1½-inch (4-cm) squares with a knife. Let it cool completely before breaking the brittle along the score lines.

SUKHADHI

Sukhadhi, also known as gur papdi, is a sweet made with durum wheat flour and jaggery that is popular in the state of Gujarat in India. Every family has their own recipe in which they add a mixture of nuts, white poppy seeds and/or shredded coconut. Feel free to add additional spices, or a mixture of nut powders to make this dish yours.

MAKES
2 DOZEN

½ cup (120 ml) ghee, melted, plus more for greasing

½ cup (72 g) jaggery powder

1 cup (128 g) durum wheat flour or whole wheat flour

½ cup (51 g) almond meal

¼ cup (27 g) unsweetened finely shredded coconut

¼ tsp ground ginger

¼ tsp ground cardamom

Grease a 9 x 9-inch (23 x 23-cm) baking pan with ghee and set aside. Add the melted ghee to a large nonstick saucepan over medium-high heat. Once the ghee is hot, add the jaggery and stir continuously until all of the jaggery has melted; this should take about 2 minutes. When the ghee and jaggery mixture foams up, add the flour while stirring continuously. Decrease the heat to low and add the almond meal, shredded coconut, ginger and cardamom. Use a spatula to mix until well combined.

Spoon the mixture into the greased baking pan and use a spatula to press the mixture into an even layer into the bottom of the pan. Cool for 15 minutes and cut the Sukhadi into 1-inch (2.5-cm) squares. Let the Sukhadhi cool completely in the pan before removing and enjoying.

ORANGE, ALMOND AND DATE BITES

If you're looking for healthy dessert recipe, I am giving you one right here. This bite is a cross between a nut bar and a praline. The maple syrup and honey mixture caramelizes and hardens slightly, giving you a crunchy, nutty bite with just a hint of sweetness. Perfect for your next hiking trip!

MAKES
3 DOZEN

1½ cups (275 g) raw almonds

¼ cup (36 g) raw cashews

4 Medjool dates, chopped small

¼ cup (41 g) raisins

½ tbsp (3 g) orange zest

¼ cup (60 ml) honey

¼ cup (60 ml) maple syrup

¼ tsp kosher salt

Preheat the oven to 350°F (177°C). Line a 9 x 9-inch (23 x 23–cm) baking pan with parchment paper.

In a large mixing bowl, add the almonds, cashews, chopped dates, raisins, orange zest, honey, maple syrup and salt. Mix well and spoon onto the parchment-lined baking pan.

Use a spatula to tightly pack and press the mixture into an even layer. Bake for 30 to 35 minutes and cool completely. Cut into 1½-inch (4-cm) square bars. Store in an airtight container at room temperature for up to 3 weeks.

COOKIES & BARS

Baking is where the true fusion of East and West occurs. The majority of baked goods were brought over to India by the Dutch, English and Portuguese. Early on, bakeries were set up to cater to the population of colonists. For example, Nankhatai (page 88), which means "bread biscuit," is a shortbread cookie that originates from my home state of Gujarat and is a product of the Dutch-Indian colonization. A Dutch bakery was set up to cater to the needs of the Dutch colonists, and eventually, Indian spices found their way into their baked goods. Nowadays, nankhatai is as Indian as it gets!

The recipes from this chapter are more fusion than traditional. It's a collection of British and American classics with Indian spices. More importantly, these cookies bring a sense of nostalgia. Each cookie in this chapter reminds me of my childhood in one way or another. For example, Bourbon Biscuits (page 74), a chocolate sandwich biscuit from England, remind me of having milk and cookies with my sister in the summertime, while Thandai Cake Rusks (page 85) remind me of many mornings where I stuffed my face with cake rusks dipped in chai as fast as I could for breakfast, so I could get to school on time! Maybe they'll bring back some memories for you too!

BOURBON BISCUITS

If you mention Bourbon Biscuits to any Indian, you'll see their eyes light up. It's two rich chocolate shortbreads sandwiched with intense chocolate buttercream. A sweet treat introduced to India in the 1950s by the British, it was initially only eaten during special occasions. These chocolate sandwich cookies are now in every family's pantries, ready for tea time. By the way, these biscuits don't contain any bourbon; they're just named after the Royal House of Bourbon.

MAKES
3 DOZEN SANDWICH COOKIES

BISCUITS
2¼ cups (280 g) all-purpose flour

½ cup (64 g) cornstarch

⅔ cup (57 g) cocoa powder

¼ tsp kosher salt

1 cup (227 g) unsalted butter, room temperature

1 cup plus 1 tbsp (215 g) granulated sugar

½ cup (120 ml) whole milk

2 tbsp (28 g) Demerara or raw sugar

CHOCOLATE FILLING
½ cup (114 g) unsalted butter, room temperature

3 tbsp (16 g) unsweetened cocoa powder

2 cups (240 g) powdered sugar

¼ tsp kosher salt

To make the biscuits, sift together the flour, cornstarch, cocoa powder and salt in a small bowl. Set aside.

In a separate bowl, cream the butter and granulated sugar together for 2 minutes. Add the dry ingredients and mix until you have a sandy, crumbly mixture. Add the milk in two additions, mixing well in between. The cookie dough should be soft but should not stick to your hands. Wrap the dough in plastic wrap and refrigerate for 15 minutes.

Roll the dough out onto a piece of parchment paper until it is ¼ inch (6 mm) thick. Slide the sheet of dough onto a baking sheet and place in the freezer for 10 minutes. Cut the dough into 1 x 2-inch (2.5 x 5-cm) rectangles and place the cookies back into the freezer for 10 minutes. This will make it easier for you to pick up the cookies and place them on the baking sheet without ruining the shape.

Place each cookie 1 inch (2.5 cm) apart onto a parchment-lined baking sheet. Take any of the scraps, roll it out again and continue cutting out cookies until all of the cookie dough has been used. Dock, or poke, each cookie with a fork and sprinkle with Demerara sugar. Place the baking sheet with the cookies in the freezer for 30 minutes.

Preheat the oven to 350°F (177°C). Bake the cookies for 12 to 15 minutes. Let the cookies cool on the baking sheet for 10 minutes before transferring them to a rack to completely cool.

While the cookies cool, make the filling. In a small bowl, add butter, cocoa powder, powdered sugar and salt. Mix well until you have a smooth, creamy filling. There are two ways to assemble the cookies. You can use a butter knife to spread the chocolate filling, or use a sandwich bag/piping bag and pipe the filling onto the cookies. Spread the chocolate filling onto half of the cookies and then top with another cookie. Store in an airtight container in the fridge or cool place for up to 1 week.

KOPRA PAK MACAROONS

My dad only knows how to make one dessert and it's kopra pak, a coconut and cardamom sweet similar to coconut burfi. When I first visited my parents in New Jersey after my daughter was born my dad made me a whole plate of kopra pak, knowing that it's one of my all-time favorite sweets and it's good for breastfeeding moms! Fun fact: coconut is lactogenic and helps increase your breast milk supply! These cookies are crunchy on the outside and soft in the middle, kind of like my dad.

MAKES
15 COOKIES

MACAROONS

1 tbsp (15 ml) heavy cream

¼ tsp saffron

2 cups (186 g) unsweetened shredded coconut

½ tsp freshly ground cardamom seeds

½ tsp kosher salt

¾ cup (150 g) granulated sugar

2 egg whites

¼ cup (60 ml) coconut oil, melted

MAWA

1¼ cups (115 g) milk powder

6½ tbsp (100 ml) heavy cream

CHOCOLATE

¾ cup (200 g) dark chocolate morsels

1 tbsp (14 g) coconut oil

3 tbsp (24 g) chopped shelled roasted pistachios

Preheat the oven to 325°F (163°C). Line a baking sheet with parchment paper.

For the macaroons, add the cream and saffron to a small bowl and stir. Set aside.

To make the mawa, add the milk powder and heavy cream to a bowl and mix well until you have a ball of dough. Place the mawa dough ball into 2 layers of cheesecloth and wrap well. Create a steamer by filling a saucepan with 2 inches (5 cm) of water and placing a strainer or steamer basket into the saucepan. Make sure the water is not touching the bottom of the basket/strainer. Place the cheesecloth-wrapped mawa dough into the steamer. Steam for 10 minutes. Remove and cool.

Using your hands, crumble the mawa into a medium mixing bowl. Add the saffron-cream mixture and mix well. In a separate bowl, add the shredded coconut, cardamom, salt and granulated sugar and stir well. Add the mawa mixture, egg white and coconut oil to the shredded coconut, and mix until you have a sticky dough.

Using an ice cream scoop, pack the macaroon mixture into the scoop and drop rounded scoops of the macaroon dough onto the parchment-lined baking sheet. Bake for 12 to 15 minutes, just until the coconut starts to turn golden brown. Rest on the baking sheet for 10 minutes before moving the macaroons to cool completely on a rack.

Add the chocolate and coconut oil to a small microwavable bowl, and microwave in 15-second increments, stirring between each increment, until all of the chocolate is melted, about 2 minutes. Alternatively, if you don't have a microwave, set up a bain-marie by bringing a small pot of water to a boil and placing a small bowl on top of the pot, making sure the bowl does not touch the water. Add the chocolate and coconut oil to the bowl and stir until melted, about 3 minutes.

Dip each macaroon into the chocolate, shake off any excess chocolate and place on the same parchment-lined baking sheet. Spoon the rest of the chocolate into a sandwich bag and snip off a small tip. Drizzle the chocolate onto the macaroons. Sprinkle the top of each macaroon with pistachios. Place the macaroons in the fridge for 10 minutes or until the chocolate has set. Enjoy immediately or store in an airtight container for up to 3 days.

CARAMELIZED WHITE CHOCOLATE AND TOASTED MILK COOKIES

These are the cookies I want my daughter to grow up with. Every mom has a dessert recipe that they share with their kids, and this is mine. This recipe was inspired by Jaques Torres's infamous chocolate chip cookie recipe to which I added an Indian twist. These cookies have a milk-y sweet flavor that comes from the toasted milk powder and caramelized white chocolate.

MAKES
2 DOZEN

1 cup (126 g) white chocolate morsels

¾ cup (69 g) instant nonfat dry milk powder

¾ cup (120 g) bread flour

1 cup (120 g) cake flour

¾ tsp baking powder

½ tsp baking soda

¾ tsp salt

¾ cup (170 g) unsalted butter, softened

⅓ cup (66 g) granulated sugar

¼ cup (55 g) light brown sugar

½ cup (72 g) jaggery powder or dark brown sugar

½ tsp cardamom seeds, finely ground

2 eggs

1 tsp vanilla extract

1 cup (108 g) slivered almonds

½ cup (50 g) chopped unsalted shelled pistachios

Flaky sea salt

Preheat the oven to 300°F (149°C) and line a 9 x 13-inch (23 x 33-cm) baking pan with parchment paper. Fit your stand mixer with a paddle attachment.

Add the white chocolate to a microwavable bowl, and microwave in 15-second increments, stirring between each increment, until all of the chocolate is melted, about 2 minutes. Alternatively, if you don't have a microwave, set up a bain-marie by bringing a small pot of water to a boil and placing a small bowl on top of the pot, making sure the bowl does not touch the water. Add the white chocolate to the bowl and stir until melted, about 5 minutes. Remove the chocolate from the heat. Add the instant nonfat dry milk powder and mix well. Spoon this mixture onto the parchment-lined baking pan and spread into a thin layer. Bake for 13 to 15 minutes or until golden brown. Let cool on the baking sheet.

In a medium mixing bowl, whisk together the bread flour, cake flour, baking powder, baking soda and salt. Set aside.

In a large stand mixer bowl, add the butter, granulated sugar, brown sugar, jaggery and cardamom. Cream the butter, sugars and cardamom on medium speed until light and fluffy, about 3 minutes. Add the eggs, one at a time, mixing in between each addition, scraping down the bowl as needed. Add in the vanilla and mix. Add the dry ingredients and mix on low until the dough just comes together. Fold in the caramelized white chocolate mixture, slivered almonds and pistachios until evenly distributed. Press plastic wrap against the dough, making sure it is completely covered, and refrigerate for at least 24 hours, or as long as 72 hours.

When ready to make the cookies, preheat the oven to 350°F (177°C) and line a baking sheet with parchment paper. Take 2 tablespoons (42 g) of the dough and roll it into a ball and place on the parchment-lined baking sheet 2 inches (5 cm) apart. Sprinkle the cookie dough balls lightly with a bit of flaky sea salt. Bake for 14 to 16 minutes. Rotate the baking tray 180 degrees halfway through baking. Allow the cookies to cool on the baking sheet for 10 minutes, then move them to a rack to cool completely. Store in an airtight container at room temperature for up to 3 days.

PISTACHIO FLORENTINES WITH WHITE CHOCOLATE

It's hard to find an Indian sweet that doesn't have a sprinkle of chopped pistachios on it. It's colorful, adds texture and is considered a treat in India due to the cost. In this cookie I use more than a sprinkle and created a cookie that highlights pistachios. Whenever I have days where all of my recipes fail, I turn to florentines to make myself feel better. This recipe is reliable and consistent: it always works. This is the kind of recipe that needs to be in everyone's recipe box. These lacy cookies look so fancy and impressive. They are delicious crumbled on top of ice cream or with a cup of coffee.

MAKES
30 FLORENTINES

1 cup (123 g) shelled unsalted roasted pistachios

5 tbsp (65 g) granulated sugar

2 tbsp (30 ml) honey

3 tbsp (45 ml) heavy whipping cream

Pinch of salt

1 cup (210 g) white chocolate melts

1 tbsp (2 g) dried rose petals, optional

Chop the pistachios and set aside.

In a small saucepan, add the granulated sugar, honey, heavy whipping cream and salt. Place over medium heat and stir continuously until the mixture hits 244°F (118°C). If you don't have a thermometer, it's about 20 seconds after it comes to a boil. Remove the saucepan from the heat and stir in the chopped pistachios. Mix well. Spoon the batter into a bowl and set aside to cool for at least 30 minutes.

Preheat the oven to 350°F (177°F) and line a baking sheet with parchment paper. Once the batter is cool, place teaspoon-size balls of dough onto a baking sheet about 3 to 4 inches (8 to 10 cm) apart. Wet your fingers with water and gently flatten each cookie so that it is 1 inch (2.5 cm) in diameter. Bake the cookies for 7 to 9 minutes. Remove from the oven and let them set for 5 minutes. Use an offset spatula to gently lift the cookies off the parchment paper and place on a rack. Bake the rest of the dough.

Add the white chocolate melts to a microwavable bowl, and microwave in 15-second increments, stirring between each increment, until all of the chocolate is melted, about 3 minutes. Alternatively, if you don't have a microwave, set up a bain-marie by bringing a small pot of water to a boil and placing a small bowl on top of the pot, making sure the bowl does not touch the water. Add the chocolate to the bowl and stir until melted, about 5 minutes. Remove the chocolate from the heat.

Use a pastry brush to brush melted chocolate onto the bottom of each cookie and set on a parchment-lined baking tray. Place the tray in the fridge for 5 minutes to set the chocolate. Spoon the rest of the remaining chocolate into a small piping bag or sandwich bag and snip off a small tip. Drizzle the chocolate over the tops of all of the cookies and sprinkle with the dried rose petals, if using. Place the tray in the fridge for 5 minutes to set the chocolate. Store in an airtight container for up to 1 week at room temperature. Enjoy!

MANGO LASSI FRENCH MACARONS

Here's an upgrade for a drink that is on the menu of every Indian restaurant in the world. These mango lassi French macarons pack a punch of flavor and are a sure way to impress your friends! These macarons are delicate and chewy. They can be fussy to make at home, but follow my directions to the tee and you'll be able to conquer this cookie!

I recommend using kesar or Alphonso mango purée to get the best flavor possible.

MAKES
3 DOZEN MACARONS

MACARON SHELLS
1 cup minus 1 tbsp (88 g) almond flour

¾ cup (90 g) powdered sugar

2 egg whites, room temperature, divided

½ cup plus 1 tbsp (113 g) granulated sugar

1½ tbsp (23 ml) water

Orange gel food coloring

In a large mixing bowl, add the almond flour, powdered sugar and 1 egg white. Mix until it is a smooth paste and set aside. Add the other egg white to a mixing bowl of a stand mixer fitted with a whisk attachment.

In a small saucepan, add the granulated sugar and water and bring to a boil over medium heat. Stir occasionally, until all of the sugar has dissolved, about 3 minutes. Turn on the stand mixer and whisk the egg white for 1 minute on medium speed. Then turn the mixer on high speed and slowly drizzle in the sugar syrup in a thin stream. Pour the syrup in so that it hits the side of the bowl and flows into the egg white. Once all of the syrup has been poured in, add the orange gel food coloring and whisk on high for 4 minutes or until the meringue is stiff. A good way to test if your meringue is ready is to flip the bowl upside down. If the meringue stays in the bowl, it's done!

Take about 1 cup (240 ml) of the meringue and mix into the almond/powdered sugar paste until it is a smooth, loose mixture. Then add the rest of the meringue and gently fold in the meringue until the batter falls off your spatula in a ribbon and melts into the rest of the batter within 10 seconds. This takes about 50 folds.

Fill a piping bag or a freezer bag fitted with a small size 12 round piping tip with the meringue mixture. Cover baking sheets in parchment paper or a Silpat if you have one. Pipe 1½-inch (4-cm) circles by piping at a 90-degree angle (straight above) the baking sheet with even pressure and then swirling the tip as you release. Once all of the macaron shells are piped out, bang the sheet four times on the counter. This flattens the macarons and lets the air bubbles out. Now let the macarons rest for 1 to 2 hours so that they form a "skin." The "skin" of the shells will firm up and prevent the macaron from cracking, so when trapped moisture wants to get out, it leaves through the bottom of the shell, creating the lovely "feet" of the macaron. You can tell they are ready when you touch the outside lightly and it doesn't stick to your finger.

(continued)

MANGO LASSI FRENCH MACARONS (CONTINUED)

MANGO LASSI BUTTERCREAM

½ cup (113 g) unsalted butter, room temperature

1 cup (120 g) powdered sugar

2½ tbsp (38 ml) mango purée

2 tbsp (30 g) plain Greek yogurt

⅛ tsp cardamom seeds, finely ground

Pinch of salt

DECORATION

¼ cup (30 g) shelled roasted unsalted pistachios

¼ tsp clear alcohol (vodka, tequila, etc.), optional

Orange gel food coloring, optional

Preheat the oven to 325°F (163°C). Bake the macarons one tray at a time in the center rack of the oven for 8 to 10 minutes. Cool the macaron shells completely.

To make the mango lassi buttercream, add the butter to a medium bowl and whisk on high until the butter is light and fluffy, about 1 minute. Then add the powdered sugar, mango purée, yogurt, cardamom and salt. Whisk on high until you have a light fluffy buttercream. Spoon the buttercream into a piping bag and cut the bag so you have a ¼-inch (6-mm) tip. Pipe the buttercream onto half of the macaron shells. Top with the remaining macaron shells.

To decorate the macarons, add the pistachios to a blender and pulse until it is a fine powder with a few coarse pieces. You don't want any pieces that are larger than a peppercorn. Roll the edge of each macaron in the pistachio powder so that the pistachios stick to the buttercream.

In a small bowl or cup, add the clear alcohol and a tiny bit of orange gel food coloring and mix with a brush. Dip the brush into the mixture and press the brush against the edges of the bowl to remove any excess liquid. Lightly brush the top of each macaron in single stroke until the entire top of the macaron is covered. Let the macrons air dry for 15 to 20 minutes. Store in the refrigerator for up to 1 week or in the freezer for up to 3 months.

 NOTE: Let your macarons bloom by refrigerating them for at least 3 days before serving. The shells become soft and chewy over time.

THANDAI CAKE RUSKS

Growing up, cake rusks were my favorite chai accompaniment. Slightly crunchy on the outside and with a tender crumb in the middle, it is a twice-baked yellow cake, similar to biscotti. The best part is that they soak up chai without falling apart! Personally, I like to dip them in rus, kesar mango purée.

Cake rusks are a piece of India's pre-partition past. They originate from Elizabethan England and were a way of preventing food waste. The low moisture content allows the cake rusks to keep for long periods of time. They are usually served plain with a cup of chai, however, I added thandai masala and chocolate to the recipe to give the rusks a more biscotti-like feel.

MAKES
4 DOZEN CAKE RUSKS

THANDAI MASALA
½ cup (72 g) raw almonds

½ cup (50 g) raw pecan halves

½ cup (73 g) raw cashews

½ cup (70 g) raw pumpkin seeds

½ tbsp (5 g) cardamom seeds

6 tbsp (78 g) granulated sugar

½ tsp saffron

¼ tsp turmeric

1 tbsp (2 g) dried rose petals

1½ tsp (4 g) fennel seeds

¼ tsp black pepper

2 tsp (5 g) ground nutmeg

CAKE RUSK
½ cup (110 g) ghee

¼ cup (60 ml) olive oil

1 cup (200 g) granulated sugar

6 eggs

1 tsp vanilla extract

2 cups (250 g) all-purpose flour

2 tsp (7 g) baking powder

¼ tsp salt

½ cup (73 g) thandai powder

To make the thandai masala, add the almonds, pecans, cashews and pumpkin seeds to a large skillet. Toast on the stove for 2 to 3 minutes over medium heat, stirring often. Add the nuts to a blender. Add the spices and blend until you have a coarse powder. Set aside.

Preheat the oven to 355°F (180°C). Grease a 9 x 13–inch (23 x 33–cm) pan with butter and set aside.

To make the cake rusks, whisk the ghee, olive oil and granulated sugar for 2 to 3 minutes until pale and fluffy. Add the eggs in one at a time, whisking well in between each egg. Add the vanilla and whisk well. Whisk together the flour, baking powder, salt and thandai powder in a separate bowl. Add half of the dry ingredients to the wet mixture and fold in using a spatula. Add the rest of the dry ingredients and fold in until smooth.

Pour the batter into the greased pan and bake for 30 minutes. Cool on a rack for 15 minutes, then cut into ½-inch (2-cm)-thick slices. Then cut each long strip into shorter rectangles, about 4 x 2 inches (10 x 5 cm).

Lower the oven temperature to 300°F (149°C). Place the cake rusks onto a baking sheet and bake for 20 minutes. Turn the rusks over and bake again for another 20 minutes. The cake rusks should be golden brown. Cool on a rack for 15 minutes.

(continued)

THANDAI CAKE RUSKS (CONTINUED)

CHAI-SPICED CHOCOLATE

1¼ cups (227 g) dark chocolate morsels

2 tsp (10 g) coconut oil

2 tsp (5 g) ground ginger

2 tsp (5 g) ground cinnamon

1 tsp ground cardamom

½ tsp ground cloves

½ tsp ground nutmeg

To make the chai-spiced chocolate, add the chocolate and coconut oil to a microwavable bowl. Microwave in 15-second increments, mixing in between, until all of the chocolate is melted, about 3 minutes. Add the spices and mix well. Spoon the chocolate into a piping bag or sandwich bag and cut off a small tip. Drizzle the chocolate onto the cake rusks and place on a parchment-lined baking sheet. Sprinkle the top with more thandai masala and let the chocolate set at room temperature. Enjoy with a cup of chai or coffee!

 NOTE: The thandai masala recipe makes 1 cup (120 g) of masala. Store the extra masala in a jar in the refrigerator. Spoon 1 tablespoon (8 g) into a cup of warm milk for a comforting drink!

NANKHATAI

As a kid, my mother refused to buy cookies from the grocery store. Every trip would end with me eyeing brightly colored packages of cookies, hoping that today would be the day that I get to try a pecan sandy. My mom eventually gave in, but what I learned that day was that my mom makes way better cookies than the Keebler elves do! She may have had only one cookie recipe in her repertoire, but let me tell you, it was the only one she ever needed! They are buttery and crunchy, and the cardamom in the cookies made the house smell so cozy while she would bake them.

MAKES
3 DOZEN COOKIES

3 tbsp (24 g) roasted unsalted shelled pistachios

½ cup (110 g) ghee

1 cup (120 g) powdered sugar

½ tsp ground cardamom

Pinch of ground nutmeg

¼ tsp baking soda

1 tsp plain yogurt

Pinch of salt

⅔ cup (115 g) semolina

1 cup minus 2 tbsp (115 g) cake flour

Preheat the oven to 300°F (149°C). Line a baking sheet with parchment paper and set aside. Chop the pistachios into tiny pieces and set aside.

Add the ghee and powdered sugar to a mixing bowl and cream together until light and fluffy, about 3 minutes. Add the cardamom and nutmeg and whisk for 1 minute. Then add in the baking soda, yogurt and salt. Mix well. Sift in the semolina and flour. Use a spatula to bring the dough together. Knead the cookie dough for 10 seconds and then pat it into a smooth ball. Roll about 1 tablespoon (15 g) of dough into a ball and place on the parchment-lined baking sheet. Place each cookie dough ball 2 inches (5 cm) apart.

Grease the bottom of a cup with a little ghee and use the cup to gently flatten each dough ball so that it is ½ inch (1.2 cm) thick. Press the chopped pistachios into the middle of each cookie. Bake the cookies for 25 to 30 minutes or until the edges start turning golden brown. Cool on a rack and store in an airtight container for up to a week.

GHARI-STUFFED ITALIAN WEDDING COOKIES

Ghari is a unique mithai popular in the city of Surat in Gujarat. It's made from a mixture of ground nuts, ghee and mawa rolled into a ball, wrapped in dough and deep fried. Instead of wrapping the nut filling with a flatbread dough, I used cookie dough!

MAKES
1 DOZEN

GHARI

2 tbsp (16 g) shelled raw pistachios

2 tbsp (18 g) raw almonds

1 tbsp (15 g) ghee

1 tbsp (9 g) chickpea flour

¼ cup (23 g) instant nonfat dry milk powder

½ cup (100 g) granulated sugar

2 tbsp (30 ml) heavy cream

WEDDING COOKIES

½ cup (113 g) unsalted butter, softened

¼ cup (30 g) powdered sugar

¼ tsp kosher salt

1 tsp vanilla extract

¾ cup (72 g) almond meal

1¼ cups (156 g) all-purpose flour

⅓ cup (40 g) powdered sugar, for rolling

To make the ghari, add the pistachios and almonds to a blender and blend into a coarse powder. Pour into a bowl and set aside. Add the ghee to a small nonstick skillet over medium-low heat. Once the ghee has melted, add the chickpea flour and mix well. Stir continuously for 2 minutes. Add the milk powder and mix well and stir for another minute. Pour the mix into the bowl with the nut powder and mix until combined. Let the mixture cool for 5 minutes and add the granulated sugar and heavy cream.

Using your hands, knead the mixture until it has a wet sandy texture. The mixture should stay together if squeezed with your fist. If the mixture feels dry to you, then add an additional teaspoon of heavy cream until you get the correct consistency. Tightly pack a ½ tablespoon (6 g) measuring spoon with the mixture. Then use your hand to squeeze the ghari mixture into a small ball. Set the ghari onto a plate and repeat until you finish the ghari mixture. Place the plate of ghari in the freezer.

Preheat the oven to 325°F (163°F) and line a baking sheet with parchment paper. To make the wedding cookies, add the butter, powdered sugar and salt to a medium mixing bowl and whisk until well combined. Add the vanilla and almond meal and mix for 1 minute. Fold in the flour until you have a smooth cookie dough. Take 1 tablespoon (15 g) of dough, roll it into a ball and flatten it with your hands. Place a ball of the ghari mixture in the middle and fold up the edges of the cookie dough so that the ghari ball is completely covered with the cookie dough. Roll into a smooth ball and place on a parchment-lined baking pan, placing each cookie 2 inches (5 cm) apart. Repeat until you have used up all of the dough. Place the baking sheet in the freezer for 10 minutes.

Bake for 25 to 30 minutes, making sure the cookies are not browning. Cool completely. Once the cookies are cool, roll each cookie in powdered sugar. Store in an airtight container for up to 1 week.

KHARI BISCUITS

Kharis are simple puff pastry biscuits that are either sweet or savory and are served with chai. This recipe requires zero technique and very little effort for a big payoff. The khari biscuits have just a hint of sweetness so that it doesn't take away or add to the sweetness of your chai.

MAKES
16 BISCUITS

1 (10 x 15-inch [25 x 38-cm]) sheet of puff pastry

1 egg, beaten

3 tbsp (24 g) powdered sugar

¼ tsp kosher salt

½ tsp ground cinnamon

¼ tsp ground ginger

¼ tsp ground cloves

¼ tsp ground cardamom

Pinch of ground nutmeg

Preheat the oven to 400°F (204°C) and line a baking sheet with parchment paper.

Cut the puff pastry into 1¼ x 5-inch (3 x 13-cm) pieces. Gently place each piece of puff pastry dough 1 inch (2.5 cm) apart on the parchment-lined baking sheet. Brush with the beaten egg.

In a small cup, combine the powdered sugar, salt, cinnamon, ginger, cloves, cardamom and nutmeg. Mix to combine then sift the powdered sugar mixture over each puff pastry. You want a thin layer of powdered sugar on top of each piece. Bake for 15 minutes or until the puff pastry is golden brown. Cool for 10 minutes and store in an airtight container for up to 10 days. Enjoy with your morning tea or crumble over ice cream!

POMEGRANATE CURD BROWNIES

Fun fact #1: India is the largest producer of pomegranates and they are grown all year round. Fun fact #2: I love chocolate-covered pomegranate seeds, which is where my inspiration for this recipe came from. If you're a sucker for chocolate covered fruit, then these bitter dark chocolate brownies swirled with tangy pomegranate curd are right up your alley!

MAKES
1 (9 X 9-INCH [23 X 23-CM]) PAN OF BROWNIES

POMEGRANATE CURD
¼ cup (60 ml) 100% pomegranate juice

¼ cup (60 ml) fresh lemon juice

½ cup (100 g) granulated sugar

1 egg

¼ cup (60 ml) unsalted butter, melted

BROWNIES
1½ cups (180 g) all-purpose flour

¼ cup (22 g) unsweetened cocoa powder

½ tsp kosher salt

¼ cup (57 g) unsalted butter

¼ cup (55 g) ghee

½ cup (96 g) semisweet chocolate morsels

1 cup (200 g) granulated sugar

⅓ cup (48 g) jaggery powder

3 eggs

1½ tsp (7 ml) vanilla extract

½ cup (120 ml) pomegranate curd

¼ cup (40 g) dark chocolate morsels

To make the pomegranate curd, in a medium microwavable bowl, combine the pomegranate juice, lemon juice, granulated sugar and egg. Whisk until combined. Slowly pour the melted butter into the pomegranate mixture while whisking. Microwave in 1-minute increments, stirring after each minute, until the curd thickens and coats the back of a spoon and hits 185°F (85°C). This should take about 6 minutes, but the time will depend on the strength of your microwave.

If you don't have a microwave, after you have whisked in the butter, put the bowl over a saucepan of simmering water over low heat and continuously whisk the curd until it has thickened and has reached 185°F (85°C), about 5 minutes.

Pour the curd through a sieve into a large bowl to make sure it is nice and smooth. Transfer to a clean jar and refrigerate until cool. Store in the fridge for up to 3 weeks or in the freezer for up to 1 year.

Preheat the oven to 350°F (177°C). Grease a 9 x 9–inch (23 x 23–cm) baking pan with butter. To make the brownies, sift the all-purpose flour, cocoa powder and salt together in a small bowl. In a small saucepan, add the butter, ghee and semisweet chocolate morsels. Heat over low heat until you have a smooth chocolate mixture, about 3 minutes. Pour the chocolate mixture into a medium mixing bowl. Add the granulated sugar and jaggery powder and mix until well combined. Whisk in the eggs one at a time. Add the vanilla and whisk to combine. Add the dry ingredients to the wet ingredients and mix with a spatula until just combined.

Spoon the brownie batter into the greased baking pan and spread. Add dollops of the curd on top. Use a butter knife to gently swirl the curd into the batter. Bake for 25 to 30 minutes and cool completely.

While the brownies cool, melt the dark chocolate morsels. Add the chocolate to a microwavable bowl, and microwave in 15-second increments, stirring between each increment, until all of the chocolate is melted, about 1 minute. Alternatively, if you don't have a microwave, set up a bain-marie by bringing a small pot of water to a boil and placing a small bowl on top of the pot, making sure the bowl does not touch the water. Add the chocolate to the bowl and stir until melted, about 2 minutes. Spoon the melted chocolate into a piping bag. Drizzle the chocolate over the brownies and let the chocolate set, or you can keep it melty and enjoy the brownies warm!

BROWN BUTTER GHEE SHORTBREAD COOKIES

One day every summer, my mom would load up the van with my sister, my cousins and me, and take us to our local grocery store. This only meant one thing—butter was on sale at the grocery store. She'd hand us all coupons, cash and a pound (454 g) of butter and tell us all to wait in line at different checkout counters. Yes, that's right, she used us to get around the buying limit of discounted butter. We'd then go home, sit in a circle on the kitchen floor and start unwrapping an ungodly amount of butter sticks and dropping them into a large pot to make ghee.

I still do this to this day, but on a smaller scale. I like my ghee on the dark side, so I cook my butter a little longer to get brown butter ghee. This recipe will make about a pint of ghee, but it lasts forever, and I've never heard anyone complain about having too much brown butter. The shortbreads just melt in your mouth and have a rich buttery texture! Don't forget to add the caramelized milk fat to the cookies; it really makes a huge difference in taste!

MAKES
16 COOKIES

BROWN BUTTER GHEE
2 cups (454 g) unsalted butter

SHORTBREAD COOKIES
½ cup (100 g) granulated sugar

1 cup (200 g) brown butter ghee

1½ tsp caramelized milk fat (saved from the ghee recipe)

1½ tsp vanilla extract

¼ tsp salt

2 ¼ cups (300 g) all-purpose flour

To make the brown butter ghee, add the butter to a large heavy-bottomed saucepan over medium-high heat. Stirring often, let the butter melt down and simmer for 10 minutes. After 10 minutes, stir continuously over low heat. Once you see the melted butter turn a golden brown and your spatula is covered in small bits of brown/black caramelized milk fat, remove from the heat. Line a strainer with 3 layers of cheesecloth and strain the ghee into a large jar. Save the caramelized milk fat that was caught in the strainer and set aside. Let the ghee cool completely.

Preheat the oven to 325°F (163°C) and line a 9 x 9-inch (23 x 23-cm) baking pan with parchment paper. To make the shortbread cookies, add the granulated sugar, brown butter ghee, caramelized milk fat, vanilla and salt to a mixing bowl. Mix on high for 2 minutes. The mixture should be pale and fluffy. Add the flour and mix for 30 seconds or just until all of the flour is incorporated into a crumbly loose dough. Dump the crumbly mixture into the parchment-lined baking pan and press the dough into an even layer. Dock the dough with a fork. Freeze for 15 minutes.

Bake for 20 to 25 minutes or until the edges just start to brown. Remove from the oven and cool for 10 minutes. Using a serrated knife, cut into sixteen 1 x 4½-inch (2.5 x 10-cm) bars and cool completely on a rack. Store in an airtight container for up to 1 week.

LEMON FENNEL SPRITZ COOKIES

This cookie was inspired by candied fennel seeds that my mom would use as sprinkles (on ice cream, cookies, everything) when I was a kid! Every single time I would think they were regular sprinkles and then I'd bite down onto hard, crunchy, candied fennel and everything was ruined. In case you were wondering, rainbow sherbet does not go well with candied fennel. As an ode to my childhood, here is a recipe for supremely tasty fennel and lemon cookies with REAL sprinkles.

MAKES
4 DOZEN

1½ tsp (5 g) fennel seeds

1¼ cups (156 g) all-purpose flour

½ tsp baking powder

¼ cup (40 g) rainbow sprinkles

¼ tsp salt

7 tbsp (100 g) unsalted butter, softened

⅓ cup (66 g) granulated sugar

1 tbsp (10 g) lemon zest

1 egg yolk

½ tsp vanilla extract

Preheat the oven to 350°F (177°C).

Slightly crush the fennel seeds using a mortar and pestle. If you don't have one, just pour the fennel seeds into a sandwich bag and use a rolling pin to slowly roll over the fennel, with pressure, 5 to 6 times. In a medium bowl, whisk the all-purpose flour, baking powder, crushed fennel seeds, sprinkles and salt together.

In a medium bowl, cream the butter, granulated sugar and lemon zest together by whisking for 2 minutes. Add the egg yolk and vanilla and whisk for another minute. Using a spatula, slowly mix in the dry ingredients until you have a ball of dough. Add the dough to your cookie press (see Note) with your choice of disc shape and press the cookies onto an ungreased baking sheet.

Bake the cookies for 8 to 10 minutes, or until the sides just start turning golden brown. Cool the cookies on the baking sheet for 10 minutes before transferring to a rack to completely cool.

NOTE: If you don't have a cookie press, add 1½ tablespoons (23 ml) of milk to the wet ingredients and use only 1 cup (125 g) of flour. Spoon the dough into a piping bag fitted with a large star tip and pipe the cookies in rosettes or 3-inch (8-cm) lines onto an ungreased baking sheet. Place the baking sheet with the piped cookies into the fridge for 10 minutes before baking.

DATE AND FIG NEWTONS

Fig Newtons were a lunchtime favorite. I might have been the only kid in the world who got excited when seeing them in my lunchbox. Since figs are good for digestion, my mom believed they were slightly healthier than other cookies, so these were the only processed cookies allowed in the house.

My homemade versions are filled with anjeer pak, or fig burfi, instead of fig marmalade.

MAKES
2 DOZEN

COOKIE DOUGH

½ cup (113 g) unsalted butter, softened

¼ cup (55 g) dark brown sugar

2½ tbsp (23 g) jaggery powder

½ tsp baking soda

¼ tsp salt

¼ tsp ground cinnamon

2¼ tsp (11 ml) honey

1 egg

1 egg yolk

1¾ cups (221 g) all-purpose flour

DATE AND FIG FILLING (ANJEER PAK)

12 dried mission figs

6 Medjool dates

2 tbsp (30 ml) orange juice

½ cup (120 ml) apple juice

½ cup (120 ml) water

¼ tsp ground cinnamon

Pinch of salt

1½ tbsp (14 g) raw almonds

1½ tbsp (12 g) shelled raw pistachios

1½ tbsp (14 g) raw cashews

To make the cookie dough, cream together the butter, brown sugar and jaggery in a medium mixing bowl until light and fluffy, about 4 minutes. Add the baking soda, salt, cinnamon and honey and mix until well combined. Add the egg and egg yolk one at a time, mixing well in between each addition. Add the flour and combine until you have a smooth dough. Shape the dough into a disc and wrap in plastic wrap. Refrigerate the dough for 1 hour.

While the cookie dough is cooling, make the date and fig filling. Quarter the figs and dates and add them to a small saucepan. Add the orange juice, apple juice, water, cinnamon and salt. Bring the mixture to a boil and then simmer over low heat for 15 minutes while stirring occasionally.

Add the almonds, pistachios and cashews to a small skillet and toast over low heat for 4 minutes. Then add the nuts to a blender and pulse 3 to 4 times until it is a coarse mixture. Add the fig and date mixture to the blender as well and blend until you have a thick paste, about 30 seconds. Spoon the mixture into a piping bag or freezer bag and place in the refrigerator to cool.

Preheat the oven to 350°F (177°C) and line a baking sheet with parchment paper. Once the dough is cool, lightly flour your work surface and roll out half the dough into a long oval that is ¼ inch (6 mm) thick. Cut the oval into a 3½ x 12-inch (9 x 32-cm)-long rectangle. Cut a 1-inch (2.5-cm)-wide tip from the piping or freezer bag with the filling and pipe the fig and date filling down the center of the dough. Take one of the long sides of the cookie dough and fold it over the filling, then fold over the other side. Gently flatten the log with your fingers.

Cut the log into 2-inch (6-cm)-long cookies and place them, seam side down, on the parchment-lined baking sheet 2 inches (6 cm) apart. Repeat with the rest of the dough. Place the tray of cookies into the freezer for 10 minutes. Bake for 15 to 18 minutes, or until the cookies just start to brown. When they are done, immediately place the cookies into an airtight container, with a paper towel in between each layer of cookies, and close. This will help retain some of the moisture for a nice soft cookie. Let the cookies cool and sit overnight before serving.

JAGGERY PUFFED RICE CRISPIES

This recipe is a mash-up of mamra na ladva (jaggery puffed rice balls) and rice crispy treats. Since vegan marshmallows weren't invented yet when I was younger, my mom would make mamra na ladva as a healthier alternative. They're made with puffed rice (mamra) mixed in a jaggery syrup and then formed into balls, similar to popcorn balls. You can find mamra at your local Indian grocery store, but rice cereal works just as well.

MAKES
16 BARS

2 tbsp (10 g) unsalted butter, plus more for greasing pan

5 cups (90 g) puffed rice (mamra) or rice cereal

1 cup (144 g) jaggery powder

4 cups (180 g) large (vegan) marshmallows

¼ tsp ground cardamom

¼ tsp ground ginger

Pinch of salt

Grease an 8 x 8-inch (20 x 20-cm) baking pan with butter and set aside. In a large nonstick pan over medium-high heat, add the puffed rice. Mix and toast the puffed rice for 5 minutes, then pour into a large bowl. If you're using rice cereal, you can skip this step.

In the same pan, melt the butter over medium heat. Once the butter has melted, add the jaggery powder. Cook while stirring continuously until the jaggery has completely melted. Add the marshmallows and turn the heat down to medium low. Stir the mixture every so often until the marshmallows have melted. Stir in the cardamom, ginger and salt. Add the puffed rice and mix well.

Spoon the mixture into the greased pan. Use a clean spatula to press the puffed rice crispies into an even layer. Let the puffed rice crispies cool for 15 minutes before cutting into 2-inch (5-cm) squares. Store in an airtight container for up to 2 days.

CAKES & TARTS

Since baked desserts are rare in Indian cuisine, the recipes in this chapter are heavily influenced by what I believe cakes, tarts and pies would be like in India. For example, my Rose and Pistachio Cake with Swiss Meringue Buttercream (page 122) was inspired by the fact that pistachios are usually found in most desserts as a garnish, but rarely as the main ingredient since they are quite expensive.

You'll also find recipes that are more of a fusion like the Rabri Tres Leches Cake (page 106) and Basundi Fruit Tart (page 124). What I learned about cakes and tarts is that they are a labor of love. A lot of time, energy and care goes into baking them, and I can see why recipes are shared from one generation to the next. Although I'll never have a cake recipe from my great-grandmother, I'm hoping these stay in my family long after I'm gone.

RABRI TRES LECHES CAKE

The first time I had tres leches cake, the milk mixture reminded me of rabri, a dessert that is made by reducing milk down until it is thick and adding sugar and spices to it. I've been fiddling with this recipe for a while, and was inspired by my fellow MasterChef contestant, Claudia Sandoval (the winner of my season!), when she made her mouthwatering tres leches cake for an elimination challenge.

MAKES
1 (9 X 13-INCH [23 X 33-CM]) SHEET CAKE

CAKE
1⅔ cups (200 g) all-purpose flour

1 tsp baking powder

½ tsp baking soda

¼ tsp salt

2 tbsp (12 g) instant nonfat dry milk powder

⅔ cup (136 g) unsalted butter, softened

1 cup (200 g) granulated sugar

6 eggs, room temperature

1 tsp vanilla extract

1½ tbsp (12 g) shelled roasted pistachios, chopped

SOAKING MILK MIXTURE
1 cup (240 ml) whole milk

1 tsp saffron

½ tsp ground cardamom

1 cup (240 ml) heavy cream

1¾ cups (420 ml) sweetened condensed milk

1½ cups (360 ml) evaporated milk

¼ tsp rose water

WHIPPED CREAM
2 cups (480 ml) heavy whipping cream

¼ cup (23 g) powdered sugar

1 tsp vanilla extract

To make the cake, preheat the oven to 350°F (177°C) and grease a 9 x 13-inch (23 x 33-cm) cake pan. Set aside.

In a large bowl, sift together the flour, baking powder, baking soda, salt and milk powder.

In a separate large mixing bowl, cream the butter and granulated sugar together until it is nice and fluffy, about 3 minutes. Add the eggs one by one, mixing in between additions. Add the vanilla and mix for 30 seconds. Make sure to scrape down the sides of the bowl every once in a while. Add the dry ingredients to wet ingredients in three additions, mixing in between each addition. Pour the batter into the prepared baking pan and spread evenly. Bake for 25 to 30 minutes and cool completely. Use a fork to poke a bunch of holes into the cooled cake.

Make the soaking milk for the cake. In a small saucepan, add the milk, saffron and cardamom. Bring to a boil while stirring continuously over medium heat. Boil for 2 minutes. Pour the hot milk into a medium mixing bowl. Add the heavy cream, sweetened condensed milk, evaporated milk and rose water. Whisk well. Refrigerate until ready to use.

When the cake is completely cool, pour the milk mixture over the cake. It will look like a lot of liquid, but the cake will soak it all up! Place the cake in the refrigerator. Refrigerate the cake while you make the whipped cream. You can also store the cake in the fridge overnight and top it with whipped cream the next day when you're ready to serve it.

To make the whipped cream, pour the heavy cream, powdered sugar and vanilla into a mixing bowl. Whisk the cream mixture until you have stiff peaks. You can spread the whipped cream on top of the cake with a spatula or pipe it on with a piping bag. Sprinkle the top with chopped pistachios.

MASALA DOODH TIRAMISU

Masala doodh is a mixture of spices ground up and added to a glass of warm milk. On many occasions when I couldn't sleep, my mom would warm up two glasses of masala doodh and we'd sit sipping on them before heading off to bed. Tiramisu is a light and delicate dessert that lends itself to the doodh masala. The lady fingers are soaked in a chai concentrate while the custard is spiced with the doodh masala. In Gujarati, doodh masala refers to the mixture of spices and nuts, and masala doodh refers to the combination of doodh masala and milk.

MAKES
1 (9 X 9-INCH [23 X 23-CM]) PAN

MASALA DOODH (MAKES 1¼ CUPS [150 G])

¼ cup (31 g) raw almonds

¼ cup (30 g) raw cashews

¼ cup (35 g) shelled raw pistachios

¼ cup (34 g) shelled raw pumpkin seeds

½ tsp ground nutmeg

¼ tsp cardamom seeds

¼ tsp fennel seeds

4 black peppercorns

¼ tsp saffron

¼ tsp ground turmeric

2½ tbsp (31 g) granulated sugar

DIPPING LIQUID

1¼ cups (296 ml) water

4 tea bags, black tea

1 tbsp (13 g) granulated sugar

1 tbsp (15 g) doodh masala powder, plus additional for garnish

CUSTARD

3 egg yolks

½ cup (110 g) granulated sugar

1¼ cups (296 ml) heavy cream, divided

3 cups (680 g) mascarpone cheese, room temperature

36 lady finger cookies

To make the doodh masala, add the almonds, cashews, pistachios and pumpkin seeds to a small skillet over medium heat. Toast for 4 minutes while mixing occasionally. Pour the nuts into a blender. Add the nutmeg, cardamom, fennel and peppercorns to the skillet and toast for 1 minute. Pour the whole spices into the blender as well. Add the saffron, turmeric and granulated sugar and blend until you have a fine powder, about 1 minute. Pour the powder into a jar and set aside.

To make the dipping liquid, add the water, tea bags, sugar and masala powder to a small saucepan over medium heat. Bring the mixture to a boil and then simmer on low for 1 minute. Remove from heat and set aside.

To make the custard, set a small saucepan with 2 inches (5 cm) of water to a boil over medium heat. In a large mixing bowl, add the egg yolks and granulated sugar. Whisk until the mixture is pale and fluffy. Add ¼ cup (60 ml) of heavy cream to the eggs and whisk until combined. Place the mixing bowl over the saucepan with the boiling water, making sure the bottom of the bowl does not touch the water. Turn the heat down to medium low and whisk continuously for 5 minutes. Remove the bowl and whisk for 2 minutes to cool.

Add the mascarpone cheese and whisk until completely smooth. In a separate bowl, add the rest of the heavy cream (240 ml) and whisk until you have stiff peaks. Fold the whipped cream and doodh masala into the egg/mascarpone mixture.

Strain the masala doodh tea into a bowl. Quickly dip the top and bottom of the lady finger cookie into the tea and place into the pan. Repeat until the bottom of the pan is covered in soaked lady fingers. Pour half of the mascarpone cream on top of the lady fingers and spread evenly. Top with a second layer of lady fingers and top with the rest of the mascarpone cream. Cover the baking pan with plastic wrap and refrigerate for 12 hours. Sprinkle the top with additional doodh masala and serve.

NOTE: This recipe will make more doodh masala than you need. You can store the excess in the fridge for up to 3 months; add a tablespoon (15 g) of it to a glass of warm milk and let your soul relax.

GULAB JAMUN CAKE

Gulab jamun is the quintessential Indian dessert. Soft, fried dough balls dipped in a sugary sweet syrup. My Shobana kaki (dad's brother's wife) is the queen of gulab jamun. When I was young, we'd go to her house for dinner parties and she'd make homemade gulab jamun, and I had the hardest time keeping my hands away from them. A lot of people don't know it, but making gulab jamun takes a lot of skill. It's all about technique, and sadly it's a technique that I rarely get right. To make it easier to enjoy my favorite dessert, I turned it into an easy cardamom-spiced Bundt cake soaked in classic saffron sugar syrup!

MAKES
1 (10-CUP [1.2-KG]) BUNDT CAKE OR 6 MINI BUNDT CAKES

CARDAMOM POUND CAKE
1 cup (226 g) unsalted butter, softened, plus 1 tbsp (15 g) for greasing

1 cup plus 1 tbsp (215 g) granulated sugar

4 eggs

1 tsp vanilla extract

½ tsp salt

1⅔ cups (227 g) all-purpose flour

½ tsp ground cardamom

GULAB JAMUN SYRUP
1 cup (240 ml) water

1 cup (200 g) granulated sugar

3-inch (8-cm) cinnamon stick

8 cardamom pods

1 tsp saffron

2 tsp (10 ml) rose water

2 tsp (10 ml) fresh lime juice

1½ cups (180 g) powdered sugar

1 tbsp (2 g) dried rose petals, optional

Grease a Bundt pan liberally with butter. Preheat the oven to 325°F (163°C).

Add the butter and granulated sugar to a large mixing bowl fitted with a paddle attachment. Mix on high for 3 minutes; the butter will turn pale and fluffy. Add the eggs one at a time, mixing well in between each addition. Add the vanilla and salt and mix for 30 seconds. Add the flour and cardamom. Mix until the flour is just incorporated. Spoon the batter into the Bundt pan and tap the pan on the counter 3 to 5 times to remove air bubbles. Bake for 35 to 40 minutes or until a toothpick inserted into the center of the Bundt cake comes out clean.

Ten minutes before the cake is done baking, make the syrup. Add the water, granulated sugar, cinnamon, cardamom pods and saffron to a small saucepan. Bring to a boil and simmer for 2 minutes. Remove from the heat and whisk in the rose water and lime juice. Remove the cinnamon stick and cardamom pods. Reserve ¼ cup (60 ml) of the syrup and set aside. Poke holes into the bottom of the Bundt cake with a fork. Take the rest of the syrup and pour onto the Bundt cake while it is still warm and in the pan. It will look like a lot of syrup, but the cake will soak it all up! Let the cake rest for 10 minutes and then turn onto a serving plate.

Take the reserved syrup and add the powdered sugar to make a glaze. Whisk well and pour over the Bundt cake. Sprinkle with the dried rose petals, if desired.

GHUGHRA GALETTE

Every year during Diwali, my mom and her sisters would come over to make a feast. For dessert we would make ghughra, also known as gujiya (a hand pie) filled with a mixture of khoya (ground nuts and jaggery). In the galette version, the pie crust is filled with a frangipane-like filling using the ingredients typically found in ghughra.

MAKES
1 (9-INCH [23-CM]) GALETTE

PIE CRUST
1½ cups (188 g) all-purpose flour

1½ tbsp (23 g) granulated sugar

½ tsp salt

¾ cup (170 g) unsalted butter, cold and cubed

1 egg

¼ cup (60 ml) milk, cold

GHUGHRA FILLING
2½ tbsp (24 g) raw almonds

3 tbsp (27 g) raw shelled pistachios

2½ tbsp (23 g) raw cashews

⅓ cup (68 g) unsalted butter, softened

⅓ cup (66 g) granulated sugar

1 egg, lightly beaten, reserve a tablespoon (15 ml) to brush the pastry

½ tsp vanilla extract

1 tbsp (8 g) all-purpose flour

1½ tbsp (16 g) semolina

Ice cream, fresh fruit or powdered sugar, for serving

To make the pie crust, mix the flour, granulated sugar and salt together in a large bowl. Add the butter and use your fingers to rub the butter and flour together until you get a wet-sandy texture. Add the egg and milk and use your hands to bring the dough together. Do not knead the dough too much, otherwise you'll end up with a tough crust that isn't flaky. Shape the dough into a disc and wrap in plastic wrap and freeze for 30 minutes.

To make the ghughra filling, add the almonds, pistachios and cashews to a blender and blend until you have a sand-like powder. In a separate bowl, cream the butter and granulated sugar together until light and fluffy. Add the egg and vanilla and whisk well. Stir in the nut powder, all-purpose flour and semolina. Set aside.

Preheat the oven to 400°F (204°C) and line a baking sheet with parchment paper. Place the dough on the baking sheet. Roll the pie crust out into an 11-inch (28-cm) circle that is ¼ inch (6 mm) thick. Spoon the ghughra filling into the center of the pie crust and spread it into a thin layer, leaving a 2-inch (5-cm) border of pie crust. Gently fold the edges of the crust over the filling.

Brush the pie crust with the reserved 1 tablespoon (15 ml) of beaten egg. Bake for 10 minutes, turn the temperature down to 375°F (190°C) and bake for an additional 30 to 35 minutes, or until the crust is golden brown. If the crust starts to brown too much, place a sheet of foil on top of the galette to prevent it from burning. Serve while warm or at room temperature with a big scoop of mango pista ice cream (page 19), fresh fruit or dusted with powdered sugar.

COCONUT AND JAGGERY TART WITH COCONUT-ALMOND CRUST

Before you could find coconut water in grocery stores, you had to get it the old-school way: by cracking a whole coconut. My sister and dad would share the coconut water while I snuck a few pieces of coconut meat. I'd take a soft piece of jaggery and smear it on top of the fresh coconut and eat it as a snack. Jaggery and coconut go together like peanut butter and jelly—it is the perfect pairing! Salty jaggery with sweet coconut are highlighted in this tart recipe.

MAKES
1 (9-INCH [23-CM]) TART

COCONUT AND JAGGERY FILLING
1½ cups (100 g) unsweetened finely shredded coconut

½ cup (120 ml) coconut milk

½ cup (120 ml) milk

1 tbsp (15 g) ghee

3 tbsp (27 g) jaggery powder

3 egg yolks

1 tbsp (15 g) granulated sugar

2 tbsp (16 g) cornstarch

¼ tsp salt

COCONUT-ALMOND CRUST
1¼ cups (100 g) unsweetened finely shredded coconut

½ cup (51 g) almond meal

¼ cup (50 g) granulated sugar

½ tbsp (4 g) cornstarch

2 egg whites

1 tsp vanilla extract

½ tsp ground cardamom, optional

¼ tsp salt

To make the coconut and jaggery filling, add the unsweetened coconut to a skillet over medium heat. Toast the coconut while continuously stirring until it is nice and golden, about 3 minutes. Pour the coconut into a small mixing bowl. In a small saucepan, add the coconut milk, milk, ghee and jaggery. Stir the milk over medium heat until all of the jaggery dissolves into the liquid. This should take about 2 to 3 minutes. Pour the warm milk into the bowl with the toasted shredded coconut and mix well. Let the mixture cool and then refrigerate for 4 hours up to overnight.

When you are ready to make the tart, preheat the oven to 350°F (177°C) and grease a 9-inch (23-cm) tart pan with butter. Add all of the ingredients for the crust to a medium mixing bowl and mix until the mixture is a smooth, sticky dough. Spoon the mixture into the tart pan. Wet your hands with cold water and gently press the coconut mixture evenly into the bottom and up the sides of the pan. Set the tart crust aside.

In a small bowl, whisk together the egg yolks, granulated sugar, cornstarch and salt. Add in the toasted coconut mixture from the fridge and whisk until smooth. Pour the filling into the tart crust and bake for 30 to 35 minutes. Let the tart cool at room temperature for 1 hour and then refrigerate overnight before serving.

SANDESH RICOTTA CHEESECAKE

Sandesh is a Bengali sweet made with fresh paneer. Making fresh paneer can be time consuming, and store-bought ricotta is sometimes used as a short cut. I was inspired to make this dessert by baked sandesh recipes that reminded me of Italian ricotta cheesecakes I would get at home in northern New Jersey.

MAKES
1 (9-INCH [23-CM])
CHEESECAKE

2 tsp (10 g) ghee

3¾ cups (850 g) whole milk ricotta cheese

⅓ cup (66 g) granulated sugar

5 eggs, room temperature

3 tbsp (13 g) unsweetened finely shredded coconut

2 tbsp (12 g) instant nonfat dry milk powder

1 tbsp (9 g) cornstarch

½ tsp vanilla extract

½ tsp ground cardamom

¼ tsp salt

Preheat the oven to 250°F (121°C). Grease a 9-inch (23-cm) pie plate with ghee and set aside.

In a large mixing bowl, whisk the ricotta and granulated sugar until well combined. Add the eggs one at a time, whisking well in between each addition. Add the shredded coconut, milk powder, cornstarch, vanilla, cardamom and salt and whisk for 2 minutes. Pour the mixture into the pie plate and bake for 60 to 70 minutes, or until the center of the cheesecake has set. After 45 minutes of baking, cover the cheesecake loosely with foil to prevent overbrowning. Cool the cheesecake completely and refrigerate overnight before serving.

CHAI "BISKOOT" CHEESECAKE WITH PARLE-G COOKIES

When visiting family, it's polite to offer chai and biscuits, or as my grandmother would say it, "biskoots," to your guests. The "biskoot" in question was always Parle-G cookies. It's the most famous cookie in India, stuffed in every mother's purse and dipped in every person's chai, it's a beloved cookie. The biscuits are crunchy, mildly sweet, nutty and caramel-y. The idea of having chai without a Parle-G biscuit was pretty much sacrilegious in my household. This cheesecake uses a Parle-G cookie crust with a masala chai cheesecake. You can find Parle-G cookies on Amazon or at your local Indian grocery store.

MAKES
1 (9-INCH [23-CM])
CHEESECAKE

PARLE-G COOKIE CRUST
34 (160 g) Parle-G cookies or graham crackers

½ cup (120 ml) unsalted butter, melted

¼ tsp salt

CHAI CONCENTRATE
½ cup (120 ml) water

2 tea bags, black tea

1 tea bag, green tea

½ tsp cardamom seeds, coarsely ground

2 star anise pods

½ tbsp (7 g) fresh ginger, minced

1-inch (2.5-cm) piece of cinnamon

CHAI CHEESECAKE
2 (8-ounce [453-g]) packages cream cheese, room temperature

½ cup (100 g) granulated sugar

2 eggs, room temperature

¾ cup (150 g) plain Greek yogurt

1 tbsp (9 g) cornstarch

⅓ cup (80 ml) chai concentrate

To make the Parle-G cookie crust, add the cookies to a blender and process until you have fine crumbs. Pour into a bowl and add the melted butter and salt. Mix well. Pour the mixture into the bottom of a 9-inch (23-cm) springform pan and press into an even layer.

To make the chai concentrate, add the water, black tea, green tea, cardamom, star anise, ginger and cinnamon into a small saucepan. Bring to a boil and simmer over low heat for 5 minutes. Strain into a measuring cup, and add additional water if needed so that there is ⅓ cup (80 ml) of concentrate.

Preheat the oven to 325°F (163°C). To make the cheesecake, add the cream cheese into a large bowl of a stand mixer. Using a paddle attachment, cream the cream cheese until it is smooth and fluffy. Add the granulated sugar and mix for 4 minutes on medium. Add the eggs one at a time, mixing well in between each addition. Add the Greek yogurt, cornstarch and chai concentrate, and mix for 5 minutes. Pour the batter over the crust and spread into an even layer. Tap the springform pan 4 to 5 times on the counter to get rid of any air bubbles. Bake for 40 minutes or until the center slightly wiggles when shaken. Remove from the oven and cool completely before refrigerating overnight. Serve with a dollop of whipped cream (page 20).

DESI SWEET POTATO PIE

Spice up this classic holiday dessert with cardamom and ginger. This pie is inspired by sakkariyā no halwo (sweet potato halwa), a dessert made with mashed sweet potatoes and cardamom. Sweet potatoes are my dad's favorite vegetable. He would steam them and then gather my sister and I around the dinner table to help him peel the skins off the piping hot sweet potatoes before devouring them. I can thank him for my ability to handle extremely hot plates and foods barehanded now.

MAKES
1 (9-INCH [23-CM]) PIE

PIE CRUST

1½ cups (188 g) all-purpose flour

1½ tbsp (23 g) granulated sugar

½ tsp salt

¾ cup (170 g) unsalted butter, cold and cubed

1 egg

¼ cup (60 ml) milk, cold

SWEET POTATO FILLING

3 small sweet potatoes

⅞ cup (210 ml) sweetened condensed milk

½ cup (120 ml) milk

2 eggs

2 egg yolks

½ tsp ground cinnamon, plus more for serving

¼ tsp cardamom seeds, finely ground

½ tsp ground ginger

¼ tsp salt

1 tbsp (15 g) ghee

To make the pie crust, mix the flour, granulated sugar and salt together in a large bowl. Add the butter and use your fingers to rub the butter and flour together until you get a wet-sandy texture. Add the egg and milk and use your hands to bring the dough together. Shape the dough into a disc and wrap in plastic wrap and freeze for 30 minutes.

Roll out the dough into a 12-inch (30-cm) circle. Carefully lift the crust and place it inside a pie plate. Press the crust into the sides of the pie plate. Cut off any overhang and use your fingers to crimp the sides of the pie. Place in the fridge until ready to use.

Preheat the oven to 425°F (218°C). To make the sweet potato filling, place the sweet potatoes in a large saucepan. Fill with water until the sweet potatoes are completely covered. Bring to a boil and then simmer, covered, for 20 to 25 minutes or until the sweet potatoes are fork tender. Remove the sweet potatoes from the water and cool for 15 minutes.

Peel the sweet potatoes with your fingers and place the sweet potatoes into a mixing bowl. Using a hand mixer or stand mixer, mix the sweet potatoes for 10 minutes to cool. Add the sweetened condensed milk and milk and whisk until smooth. Add the eggs and egg yolks one at a time, mixing well in between each addition. Whisk in the cinnamon, cardamom, ginger, salt and ghee.

Pour the mixture into the pie crust and tap on the counter 5 to 6 times, to get rid of any air bubbles. Bake the pie for 10 minutes, then turn down the heat to 350°F (177°C) and bake for an additional 30 minutes, or until the center is set. Cool completely and then refrigerate overnight before serving. To garnish, top with a dollop of whipped cream (page 20) and a sprinkle of cinnamon.

ROSE AND PISTACHIO CAKE WITH SWISS MERINGUE BUTTERCREAM

Whenever a family member was visiting India, we would pack their bags with tons of pistachios to give as gifts to family and friends. Nuts are very expensive in India and a bag of pistachios in India can cost up to double the amount compared to in America. This luxurious cake is made with tons of ground pistachios, then soaked in rose water sugar syrup and frosted with a light turmeric Swiss meringue buttercream.

MAKES
1 (9-INCH [23-CM]) TWO-LAYER CAKE

PISTACHIO CAKE

1 cup (226 g) unsalted butter, softened, plus more for greasing pans

2 cups (246 g) shelled roasted unsalted pistachios

1⅔ cups (240 g) cake flour

3 tsp (14 g) baking powder

½ tsp baking soda

1 tsp salt

1½ cups (300 g) granulated sugar

4 eggs, room temperature

½ cup minus 1 tbsp (100 g) sour cream

1 tbsp plus 1 tsp (20 g) plain yogurt

6 tbsp (90 g) mayonnaise

2 tsp (10 ml) vanilla extract

1 cup (240 ml) milk

ROSE SYRUP

¼ cup (50 g) granulated sugar

¼ cup (60 ml) water

¼ tsp rose water

Preheat the oven to 350°F (177°C) and grease two 9-inch (23-cm) round cake pans with butter and line with parchment paper.

To make the pistachio cake, add the pistachios to a blender and blend until they are a fine powder. Add the pistachio powder to a mixing bowl. Add the cake flour, baking powder, baking soda and salt and whisk well.

In a separate mixing bowl, cream the butter and granulated sugar together using a stand mixer or handheld mixer for 5 minutes, until light and fluffy. Add the eggs one at a time, mixing well in between each addition. Add the sour cream, yogurt, mayonnaise and vanilla, and mix until well combined. Alternately add the dry ingredients and milk in four batches, mixing in between each addition. Scrape down the bowl every once in a while, to make sure you have a smooth batter.

Divide the batter into the two greased cake pans—about 3½ cups (818 g) of batter per pan. Tap the pans onto the counter 3 to 4 times to get rid of any air bubbles. Bake the cakes for 25 to 30 minutes, or until a toothpick that is inserted in the center comes out clean. Let the cakes cool for 5 minutes and then flip the cakes out onto a rack to cool completely. Trim the edges and tops of each cake so that they are level. Keep the trimmings and crumble them into a small bowl.

To make the rose syrup, add the granulated sugar and water to a small saucepan over medium heat. Stir until all of the sugar dissolves. Pour the simple syrup into a small bowl and stir in the rose water. Set aside to cool.

TURMERIC SWISS MERINGUE BUTTERCREAM

½ tsp turmeric powder

4 egg whites

1 cup (200 g) granulated sugar

1¾ cups (396 g) unsalted butter, softened

¼ tsp salt

2 tbsp (16 g) shelled roasted unsalted pistachios, chopped

1 tbsp (2) dried rose petals, optional

To make the turmeric Swiss meringue buttercream, add the turmeric, egg whites and granulated sugar into a large mixing bowl. Set a saucepan filled with 2 inches (5 cm) of water over medium heat and bring it to a simmer. Once it simmers, set the bowl of egg whites over the pan, making sure the water doesn't touch the bottom of the bowl.

Turn the heat down to low and continuously whisk until the mixture hits 160°F (71°C). Remove the mixing bowl from the heat and whisk the egg mixture on high for 10 minutes, until it is a light, fluffy meringue and the bowl is cool. Slowly add the butter a tablespoon (15 g) at a time while mixing until all of the butter has been incorporated. Use a spatula to scrape down the bowl every once in a while.

Place one layer of cake down on a plate or turntable. Using a pastry brush, brush the cake with half of the rose syrup. If you don't have a pastry brush, you can drizzle the syrup on with a spoon. Spread about 1 cup (220 g) of the buttercream over the top of the cake so you have a ½-inch (1-cm)-thick layer of buttercream. Gently place the next cake layer on top of the buttercream frosting.

Brush the top of the second layer with the rest of the rose syrup. Using an offset spatula, frost the top and sides of the cake with a thin layer of buttercream; this is called a crumb coat. Chill the cake for about 30 minutes in the refrigerator. Finish frosting the cake with the remaining buttercream. Press the leftover cake crumbs on the bottom of the cake. Sprinkle the chopped pistachios and dried rose petals, if using, on the top of the cake. Refrigerate until ready to serve.

BASUNDI FRUIT TART

A dinner party at the Sheladia household was never complete without basundi, or as we like to call it, fruit salad, pronounced "phroot salaad." Basundi is milk that is reduced down until it is fatty and thick, then spiced with saffron and cardamom.

MAKES
1 (9-INCH [23-CM]) TART

CRUST
1¼ cups (156 g) all-purpose flour, plus more for work surface

1½ tbsp (20 g) granulated sugar

¼ tsp salt

½ cup (113 g) unsalted butter, cold and cubed

1 tbsp (15 ml) ice-cold water

BASUNDI FILLING
2 cups (480 ml) whole milk

¼ tsp cardamom seeds, finely ground

½ tsp vanilla extract

4 egg yolks

½ cup (100 g) granulated sugar

¼ cup (35 g) cornstarch

Pinch of salt

2 tbsp (28 g) unsalted butter, softened

¼ tsp saffron

TOPPING
2 cups (246 g) fresh raspberries (see Note)

2 cups (296 g) fresh blueberries

2 tbsp (20 g) slivered almonds

To make the crust, add the all-purpose flour, granulated sugar, salt and butter into a medium bowl. Use a fork to cut the butter into the flour until you have a sandy texture. Add the ice-cold water and mix until it just comes together into a ball of dough. If the dough is too dry, add an additional tablespoon (15 ml) of water and mix. Press the dough into a thick disc, about 5 inches (13 cm) wide and wrap with plastic wrap. Refrigerate for 15 minutes. Lightly flour your surface and roll out the dough until it is ¼ inch (6 mm) thick and about 15 inches (38 cm) wide. Dust your rolling pin with some flour and carefully roll the crust around it. Then unroll it over a 9-inch (23-cm) tart pan. Gently press the crust into the tart pan and cut off any excess dough. Dock the sides and bottom with a fork and freeze the crust for 30 minutes.

Preheat the oven to 325°F (163°C). Press a sheet of foil into the crust and fill with uncooked rice or beans. This will help make sure the crust doesn't puff up. Bake for 10 minutes and remove the foil and rice. Bake for an additional 25 minutes. Cool completely.

To make the basundi filling, add the milk, cardamom and vanilla into a small saucepan. Heat over medium heat until bubbles start forming on the edges of the milk. Turn the heat off. In a medium bowl, add the egg yolks, granulated sugar, cornstarch and salt. Whisk for 5 minutes until it is pale.

Temper the yolks by adding ½ cup (120 ml) of the hot milk to them. Whisk continuously for 1 minute to prevent the yolks from cooking. Pour the egg mixture into the saucepan with the rest of the milk. Add the butter and cook the filling over medium-high heat while whisking continuously. The filling will thicken as the cornstarch is activated by the heat. This should take about 3 to 4 minutes. Once the custard gets thick, cook for 1 minute and remove from the heat. Pour the filling through a sieve into a bowl. Stir in the saffron and place a piece of plastic wrap directly on top of the cream to prevent a skin from forming. Refrigerate the filling until cool.

When the basundi filling is cool, spoon it into the baked tart crust and spread evenly. Decorate with raspberries, blueberries and slivered almonds. Refrigerate until ready to serve.

 NOTE: Use fruits that are local and seasonal to you. Mangos, sliced bananas, strawberries and grapes are perfect with the tart!

LEMON AND BLACKBERRY POKE CAKE

There is a famous bakery in Bangalore that makes an eggless cake that is glazed with honey and covered in strawberry jam and shredded coconut, almost like a one-layer Victoria sponge cake. Mix that with an American classic like the poke cake, a boxed cake poked with holes and topped with Jell-O and whipped cream, you get my lemon and blackberry poke cake!

MAKES
1 (9 X 9-INCH [23 X 23-CM]) CAKE

CAKE

1 tbsp (8 g) lemon zest

1½ cups (300 g) granulated sugar

1 cup (257 g) plain yogurt

¾ cup plus 2 tsp (190 ml) vegetable oil

1¼ tsp (6 ml) vanilla extract

1 tbsp (15 ml) lemon juice

¼ cup (60 ml) whole milk

3⅓ cups (424 g) cake flour

¼ tsp baking soda

1¼ tsp (5 g) baking powder

¼ tsp salt

1 tbsp (6 g) unsweetened finely shredded coconut

BLACKBERRY-HONEY SAUCE

2 tbsp (30 ml) water

⅓ cup (80 ml) honey

¾ cup (30 g) blackberry jam

COCONUT WHIPPED CREAM

1 (14-oz [396-g]) can of coconut cream or full-fat coconut milk, refrigerated overnight

¼ cup (30 g) powdered sugar

½ tsp vanilla extract

¼ cup (36 g) fresh blackberries

Mint leaves, optional

Preheat the oven to 355°F (180°C). Line a 9 x 9-inch (23 x 23-cm) pan with parchment paper and grease with cooking spray.

In a large mixing bowl, add the lemon zest and granulated sugar. Use your fingers to rub the zest and sugar together until the sugar turns pale yellow. Add the yogurt, vegetable oil, vanilla, lemon juice and whole milk and whisk for 3 minutes or until well combined. Sift in the cake flour, baking soda, baking powder and salt. Fold the dry ingredients into the wet ingredients until the batter is smooth. Pour the batter into the greased baking pan and bake for 40 to 45 minutes or until a toothpick inserted in the center of the cake comes out clean. Let the cake cool for 5 minutes. Poke holes that are 1 inch (2.5 cm) deep into the cake that are 2 inches (5 cm) apart with the bottom of a wooden spoon.

While the cake is baking, make the blackberry-honey sauce. Add the water, honey and blackberry jam to a small saucepan over medium heat. Mix well and bring the mixture to a boil and simmer for 2 minutes.

While the cake is warm, pour the warm blackberry sauce on top of the cake and spread evenly, making sure the sauce gets into all of the holes in the cake. Sprinkle with the shredded coconut and let the cake cool completely.

Make the coconut whipped cream. If using full-fat coconut milk, open the can and drain away any of the liquid. Add the coconut cream to a bowl with the powdered sugar and vanilla. Whisk well until you have a light, airy whipped cream. Spread the coconut whipped cream on top of the cooled cake into an even layer. Decorate with fresh blackberries and mint leaves, if using. Refrigerate the cake for 1 hour before serving.

JAGGERY AND COCONUT CRÊPE CAKE

Patishaptas are Bengali crêpes made with semolina and rice flour which are filled with a sticky coconut and jaggery filling. The rice flour gives them a mochi-like chewy texture that I personally love. To make my spin on this dessert I layered patishaptas and a coconut whipped cream into a tall crêpe cake. This crêpe cake is a labor of love and takes some time to make (it's 25 crêpes!), but well worth the effort!

MAKES
1 (9-INCH [23-CM]) CRÊPE CAKE

PATISHAPTA BATTER

1½ cups (188 g) all-purpose flour

¼ cup (42 g) semolina

2 tbsp (18 g) rice flour

2 tbsp (30 g) granulated sugar

Pinch of salt

¾ cup (180 ml) coconut milk

2 cups (480 ml) water

1 tsp ghee, for cooking

COCONUT WHIPPED CREAM

2 cups (480 ml) heavy whipping cream

½ cup (72 g) jaggery powder

¾ cup (74 g) unsweetened finely shredded coconut

¼ tsp ground cardamom

2 tbsp (30 ml) sweetened condensed milk

To make the patishaptas, whisk together the all-purpose flour, semolina, rice flour, granulated sugar, salt, coconut milk and water until smooth in a bowl. Heat a small nonstick skillet over medium-high heat. Coat a 9-inch (23-cm) skillet with 1 teaspoon of ghee and pour ⅓ cup (80 ml) of the batter into the center of the pan. Swirl the skillet to evenly spread the batter. Cook for 30 seconds, flip and cook an additional 15 seconds. Lay the crepes out on a flat surface until they are all cool. Continue with the rest of the batter.

To make the coconut whipped cream, pour the heavy whipping cream into a mixing bowl. Add the jaggery and whisk until stiff peaks form, about 4 to 5 minutes with a handheld mixer. Add the coconut, cardamom and sweetened condensed milk and whisk for 2 minutes.

Lay down one crêpe and spread about 2 to 3 tablespoons (30 to 45 ml) of the whipped cream into a thin even layer on top of the crêpe. Lay another crêpe on top and spread whipped cream on top. Repeat until all of the crêpes are used. Refrigerate the crêpe cake for at least 2 hours before serving.

APRICOT RASPBERRY MAWA CAKE

Mawa cake is a traditional yellow cake featuring mawa, or milk fat, made by boiling milk down until all of the liquid has evaporated. To shorten the process, I use dry nonfat milk powder mixed with ghee and milk. It's a simple shortcut that cuts hours off the cooking time. The mawa give a moist cake that has a milky taste to it, similar to Japanese milk breads. Traditionally mawa cakes are topped with nuts; however, I added fresh apricots and raspberries to cut the denseness of the cake. This is a great tea cake since it's mildly sweet and buttery.

MAKES
1 (9-INCH [23-CM]) CAKE

½ cup (113 g) unsalted butter, softened, plus more for greasing pan

1 cup plus 1 tbsp (133 g) all-purpose flour

¾ tsp baking powder

¼ tsp salt

⅓ cup plus ¾ cup (260 ml) whole milk, divided

¾ cup (69 g) nonfat instant milk powder

1½ tbsp (23 g) ghee

1 cup (200 g) granulated sugar

1 egg

1 egg yolk

1 tsp vanilla extract

2 apricots, sliced

1 cup (123 g) raspberries

Powdered sugar, for dusting

Preheat the oven to 350°F (177°C). Grease a 9-inch (23-cm) springform pan with butter and set aside.

Add the flour, baking powder and salt to a small mixing bowl and whisk well. Set aside.

Make the mawa by adding ⅓ cup (80 ml) of milk to a small nonstick skillet over medium heat. Add the milk powder and ghee and mix for 2 minutes. Pour the mawa into a stand mixer bowl. Fit the mixer with a paddle attachment and mix the milk mixture for 5 minutes on high to cool the mixture down.

Add the butter and granulated sugar to the mawa mixture and cream on high for 4 minutes. Add the egg, egg yolk and vanilla, and mix until combined. Alternately, add the remaining milk and dry ingredients in 3 additions, mixing in between each addition. Pour the batter into the prepared baking pan and smooth into an even layer. Arrange the sliced apricots and raspberries on top of the batter. Bake the cake for 45 to 50 minutes, or until a toothpick inserted in the middle of the cake comes out clean. Cool completely. Dust with powdered sugar before serving.

PINEAPPLE UPSIDE DOWN BAATH CAKE

Pineapple and coconut, a beloved tropical combination, in cake form! Baath cake is a Goan semolina and coconut cake that is traditionally made during Christmas time. This cake is said to have been brought over by the Portuguese, who had a huge influence over the food and culture of Goa. There are other variations of this cake found in countries that used to be a part of the Portuguese empire. This version is a mash-up of pineapple upside down cake and baath cake.

MAKES
1 (9 X 9-INCH [23 X 23-CM]) CAKE

CAKE

¼ cup (57 g) unsalted butter, softened

1 cup (200 g) granulated sugar

2 eggs

1 egg yolk

½ tsp vanilla extract

1 cup plus 2 tbsp (270 ml) coconut milk

¼ cup (60 ml) pineapple juice

1 tbsp (15 ml) rose water

1 cup (167 g) semolina

¼ cup (31 g) all-purpose flour

¼ tsp salt

¼ tsp baking powder

3½ tbsp (22 g) unsweetened finely shredded coconut

CARAMEL

¼ cup (57 g) unsalted butter

½ cup (110 g) light brown sugar

6 pineapple slices

To make the cake, add the butter and granulated sugar to a large mixing bowl and cream for 5 minutes. Add the eggs, egg yolk and vanilla and whisk for 3 minutes until the batter is smooth. Add the coconut milk, pineapple juice and rose water and mix until incorporated. Add the semolina, all-purpose flour, salt, baking powder and shredded coconut and mix until just combined. Cover the bowl with plastic wrap and refrigerate the batter for at least 5 hours; overnight is best.

Preheat the oven to 350°F (177°C). Grease a 9 x 9-inch (23 x 23-cm) baking pan with butter and set aside. For the caramel, add the unsalted butter and brown sugar to a small saucepan over medium heat. Bring to a boil and them simmer over low heat for 2 minutes. Pour the caramel into the bottom of the baking pan. Tilt the pan so that the caramel coats the bottom of the entire pan. Arrange the pineapple slices on top of the caramel. Cut 1 slice of pineapple into smaller pieces to fit into the open gaps.

Pour the batter on top and smooth it into an even layer with a spatula. Bake for 40 to 50 minutes, or until a toothpick inserted in the center of the cake comes out clean. Cool for 15 minutes. Take a knife and run it along the edges of the cake. Place a serving plate on top of the cake and flip it. The cake should easily come out of the baking pan. Serve while warm or room temperature with a cup of tea or coffee.

BREADS & JAMS

In my household, fresh bread was made daily. A variety of flatbreads like roti, paratha, bhakri, puri and naan were made by hand at home. Indian breads are typically savory. Because of this, the recipes in this chapter are more American/European than Indian. I'd like to think that this is a progression of Indian desserts. As you can see in my other chapters, so many of the desserts in India were influenced by colonization, immigration or trade. This chapter is just a continuation of what's been happening for hundreds of years. People travel and learn new recipes and dishes and apply them to what they know. Indians took shortbreads and turned them into nankhatai, and now I'm taking traditional sweet breads and adding my spin to them.

Jams, on the other hand, are a traditional part of most Indian meals. Chhundo (Green Mango Marmalade [page 151]), a sweet and savory marmalade made with tart green mangos, was my favorite bread accompaniment. It's tart, salty and sweet with a hint of spice that pairs so well with flatbreads and sharp cheeses! Murrabas are sweet fruit preserves that were brought over to India through the Middle East; the most famous being Khubani Ki Murraba, or Apricot Murraba (page 152). Jams are enjoyed with almost every meal and the recipes I share combine the traditional flavors I grew up with with modern cooking techniques.

ORANGE AND CARDAMOM CINNAMON ROLLS

I had family members who worked at a famous donut chain on the East Coast and would bring home boxes and boxes of donuts and cinnamon buns. Weekend breakfasts consisted of warmed-up cinnamon rolls, chai and cartoons. These cinnamon rolls are filled with orange zest and cardamom filling. I know the icing is usually the best part, but in this recipe, the bread is definitely the winner!

MAKES
1 DOZEN

DOUGH
1 cup minus 1½ tbsp (217 ml) milk

1½ tsp (6 g) active dry yeast

3 tbsp (40 g) unsalted butter, room temperature

3 tbsp (35 g) granulated sugar

1½ tsp salt

1 egg

1 egg yolk

2 cups (250 g) all-purpose flour

1¾ cups plus 1 tbsp (250 g) bread flour

Vegetable oil, for greasing bowl

FILLING
¼ cup (50 g) granulated sugar

1 tbsp (6 g) orange zest

¼ cup (55 g) dark brown sugar

3 tsp (8 g) ground cinnamon

1 tsp cardamom seeds, finely ground

¼ tsp salt

¼ cup (57 g) unsalted butter, room temperature, plus more for greasing pan

ICING
2 cups (240 g) powdered sugar

3 tbsp (45 ml) milk

1 tsp vanilla extract

In a saucepan or microwave, heat the milk until it is 110°F (43°C), lukewarm to the touch. Add yeast to the milk and stir, and set aside for 5 minutes. In a large bowl, add the butter, granulated sugar and salt. Mix well with a spatula. Then mix in the egg and egg yolk until well combined. Add the yeast/milk mixture and stir well. Using a dough hook, or your hands, slowly incorporate the flours into the wet ingredients.

Knead for 6 to 7 minutes or until the dough is soft, stretchy and tacky. Grease a large bowl with a little vegetable oil and place the dough ball into the bowl and cover with plastic wrap. Set in a warm place for 90 minutes or until the dough doubles in size.

In a small mixing bowl, mix together the granulated sugar and orange zest. Use your fingers to rub the orange zest into the sugar until the sugar is pale orange. Add the brown sugar, cinnamon, cardamom and salt and mix well. Melt the butter and set aside. Grease a 9 x 13–inch (23 x 33-cm) pan or two 9-inch (23-cm) round pans with butter and set aside.

Roll out the dough into a 15 x 12–inch (38 x 30–cm) rectangle (the dough should be ½ inch [13 mm] thick). Brush the entire rectangle with the melted butter. Then evenly sprinkle on the orange/sugar mixture over the entire rectangle.

Take the edge of the long side of the rectangle and start rolling the dough up into a tight log. Cut the log into 1¼-inch (3-mm) slices using a sharp knife. Arrange the cinnamon rolls cut side down onto the greased baking pan, leaving a 1-inch (2.5-cm) gap between each cinnamon roll. Cover the pan with plastic wrap or a tea towel and let the dough rise for 1 hour or until double in size.

Preheat the oven to 350°F (177°C). Bake the cinnamon rolls for 25 to 30 minutes or until golden brown. Cool for 15 minutes. While the cinnamon rolls are cooling, make the icing. Add the powdered sugar, milk and vanilla to a mixing bowl and whisk until smooth. Drizzle the icing onto the rolls and enjoy while warm!

BANANA CUSTARD BRIOCHE DONUTS

These soft, fluffy brioche donuts filled with thick banana custard are inspired by gulgula, or banana donuts, and my love for Amish powdered donuts. I went to college in Philadelphia, and the Amish donuts there changed my life forever. They are the softest, fluffiest donuts in the world and have ruined all other donuts for me. If you're ever in Philadelphia, grab a dozen from Reading Terminal; I promise you won't regret it!

MAKES
1 DOZEN DONUTS

BRIOCHE DONUTS
1¼ cups plus 2 tbsp (330 ml) whole milk, warm (110°F [43°C])

2 tsp (7.6 g) yeast

5½ cups (700 g) all-purpose flour, plus more for work surface

1 tsp salt

⅓ cup (66 g) granulated sugar

2 eggs

1 egg yolk

6½ tbsp (93 g) unsalted butter, room temperature

1 cup (120 g) powdered sugar

Vegetable oil, for frying

BANANA CUSTARD
1 banana

1½ cups (360 ml) whole milk

½ tsp vanilla extract

2 egg yolks

¼ cup (50 g) granulated sugar

2 tbsp (16 g) cornstarch

¼ tsp salt

To make the brioche donuts, add the warm milk and yeast to a small bowl and stir. Let this rest for 5 minutes.

Fit a stand mixer with a dough hook. In the bowl for the stand mixer, add the flour, salt and granulated sugar. Mix for 30 seconds. Add the yeast mixture, eggs and egg yolk and mix on medium speed for 10 minutes. Then add the room temperature butter while the dough is mixing, 1 tablespoon (14 g) at a time. Once the butter is incorporated, turn off the mixer and knead the dough with your hands for 2 minutes.

Place the dough into a lightly greased bowl, cover with a tea towel or plastic wrap and proof for 1½ hours, or until the dough has doubled in size. Once the dough has proofed, lightly flour your work surface and roll the dough out until it's ¾ inch (19 mm) thick. Use a 3-inch (8-cm) round cookie cutter to cut out donuts. Roll out the scraps and cut additional donuts out until all of the dough is used. If the dough keeps shrinking, let the dough rest for 5 minutes and then try rolling the dough out again. Cover the donuts with a tea towel and proof for 40 minutes.

Heat the oil in a large heavy-bottomed pan until it is 365°F (186°C). Gently drop the donuts into the oil, two at a time. Fry each side for 1½ to 2 minutes, or until both sides are golden brown. Cool the fried donuts on a rack.

For the custard, add the banana to a blender and purée until smooth. Add the banana purée, milk and vanilla to a small saucepan over medium-low heat. Heat the milk mixture until bubbles start to appear on the edges of the milk, about 3 minutes. Remove from the heat.

In a medium mixing bowl, add the egg yolks, granulated sugar, cornstarch and salt. Whisk for 5 minutes. Pour ½ cup (120 ml) of the banana milk mixture into the eggs and whisk for 30 seconds. Then add the egg mixture into the saucepan and whisk over medium-high heat for 4 to 5 minutes, or until the mixture starts to thicken. As soon as you have a thick custard, remove from the heat and push the mixture through a strainer into a clean mixing bowl. Cover the custard with plastic wrap and cool completely. Once cool, whisk the custard for 1 to 2 minutes to loosen it so that it is smooth and creamy. Spoon the mixture into a piping bag fitted with a small round tip.

Pour the powdered sugar into a shallow bowl. Use a knife to poke a hole into the side of each donut. Pipe the custard into the donuts and then roll the donuts in the powdered sugar until well coated.

BOURNVITA BABKA

Babka is traditionally made with a brioche-like dough; however I opted for a milk bread dough. This bread is made with a Japanese technique that uses tanzhong, or a roux made with bread flour and milk. It helps hydrate the flour, which leads to more steam, creating a fluffy, light bread.

MAKES
1 (9 X 5-INCH [23 X 13-CM]) LOAF OF BABKA

TANZHONG
2 tbsp (17 g) bread flour

7 tbsp (105 ml) whole milk

BREAD
⅔ cup (160 ml) whole milk

1 tbsp (15 g) granulated sugar

2½ tsp (10 g) active dry yeast

2⅓ cups (320 g) bread flour

1 egg (50 g)

1 tsp salt

1½ tbsp (21 g) unsalted butter, room temperature

BOURNVITA FILLING
6 tbsp (85 g) unsalted butter

½ cup (100 g) dark chocolate morsels

¼ cup (30 g) powdered sugar

¼ cup (22 g) unsweetened cocoa powder

¼ cup (23 g) Bournvita or malted milk powder

¼ tsp salt

To make the tanzhong, add the bread flour and milk to a saucepan over medium-low heat. Whisk together until it starts to thicken, about 30 seconds. It should be thick enough so that your whisk leaves a trail when stirring. Remove from heat and let cool.

Butter the 9 x 5-inch (23 x 13-cm) loaf pan and line with parchment paper, then set aside.

To make the bread, add the milk to a small saucepan over low heat and heat until it is 100 to 110°F (38°C to 44°C). Add the warm whole milk, granulated sugar and yeast to a small bowl and stir. Let this sit for 10 minutes to activate the yeast. Add the bread flour, egg, salt, yeast mixture and tanzhong to a mixing bowl for a stand mixer. Use a spatula to roughly mix the ingredients together. Using a dough hook on the stand mixer, mix on medium speed for 5 minutes. Scrape down the bowl with a spatula and add the butter. Mix for another 5 minutes. The dough is ready when it springs back immediately when it's poked. Cover the dough with a tea towel and place in a warm place for 1 to 1½ hours to rise, or until it has doubled in size.

When the dough is almost done rising, make the filling by adding the unsalted butter and chocolate to a saucepan over medium-low heat. Once the butter and chocolate have melted, remove from the heat and mix for 1 minute to cool down. Add the powdered sugar, cocoa powder, Bournvita powder and salt, and whisk until well combined.

Once the dough has proofed, lightly flour your surface and roll the dough into a 15 x 11-inch (38 x 28-cm) rectangle. Spread the filling mixture over the dough into a thin, even layer, leaving a ½-inch (13-mm) border along the edges. Lightly brush the edge farthest from you with water. Roll the dough up and pinch the water-brushed edge into the log of dough.

Transfer the log of dough onto the parchment-lined baking sheet and freeze for 15 minutes. Cut the log down the middle lengthwise. Lay both sides of the log cut side up. Twist the two pieces of dough by lifting one piece over the other making sure the cut side of the dough faces out. Gently place the twisted bread into the parchment-lined loaf pan. Cover with a tea towel. Let the bread rise for 1 hour or until it has doubled in size.

When you're ready to bake, preheat the oven to 350°F (177°C). Bake for 30 to 35 minutes, until the center of the bread registers at 190°F (88°C). Cool in the pan for 10 minutes. It's best served warm!

CINNAMON AND JAGGERY MONKEY BREAD

The first time I made monkey bread, it was at a Thanksgiving dinner with my entire family while I was in college. It was the first dessert I ever made for my family that didn't come out of a box! In this recipe, I use jaggery in the caramel and dusting sugar to give it a sticky molasses-y feel and taste. Monkey bread is meant to be shared and this recipe is ideal for any family gathering!

MAKES
1 (10-CUP [2.2-KG]) BUNDT

DOUGH

1 cup minus 1½ tbsp (217 ml) whole milk

1½ tsp (6 g) active dry yeast

¼ cup (57 g) unsalted butter, room temperature

3 tbsp (45 g) granulated sugar

1½ tsp (5 g) salt

1 egg

1 egg yolk

2 cups (250 g) all-purpose flour

1¾ cups plus 1 tbsp (250 g) bread flour

Vegetable oil, for greasing

CARAMEL SAUCE

½ cup (100 g) granulated sugar

½ cup (72 g) jaggery powder

½ cup (113 g) unsalted butter

¼ cup (60 ml) heavy cream

¼ tsp salt

DUSTING SUGAR

¼ cup (57 g) unsalted butter

¼ cup (50 g) granulated sugar

¼ cup (36 g) jaggery powder

2 tsp (5 g) ground cinnamon

¼ tsp salt

In a saucepan or microwave, heat the milk until it is 110°F (43°C), and lukewarm to the touch. Add the yeast to the milk and stir and set aside for 5 minutes. In a large bowl, add the butter, granulated sugar and salt. Mix well with a spatula. Then mix in the egg and egg yolk until well combined. Add the yeast/milk mixture and stir well. Using a dough hook, or your hands, slowly incorporate the flours into the wet ingredients. Knead for 6 to 7 minutes, or until the dough is soft, stretchy and tacky. Grease a large bowl with a little vegetable oil, place the dough ball into the bowl and cover with plastic wrap. Set in a warm place for 90 minutes, or until the dough doubles in size.

While the dough is rising, make the caramel sauce. Add the sugar, jaggery, butter, heavy cream and salt into a medium saucepan over medium heat. Stir until all of the butter has melted and it is a smooth sauce, about 3 minutes. Set aside.

To make the dusting sugar, melt the butter in a small bowl and set aside. In a separate bowl, whisk together the granulated sugar, jaggery, cinnamon and salt.

Grease a Bundt pan with butter and pour ½ cup (120 ml) of the caramel sauce into the bottom of the pan. Roll the dough out into a 16 x 16-inch (40 x 40-cm) square and use a knife to cut the dough into 2 x 2-inch (5 x 5-cm) squares.

Take each piece of dough and roll it into a ball. Then take each dough ball and dip it into the melted butter, shake off any excess butter and drop the dough ball into the dusting sugar mixture. Coat each dough ball with the sugar mixture and place them into the Bundt pan. Repeat until all of the dough balls are in the Bundt pan. Pour the rest of the caramel sauce over the dough balls. Cover the Bundt pan with plastic wrap and set in a warm place to proof for 30 minutes or until the dough doubles in size. With 10 minutes remaining in the proof, preheat the oven to 400°F (204°C).

Bake the bread for 15 to 17 minutes, or until it is golden brown. When done, turn the monkey bread out onto a large plate. Cool for 10 minutes before serving.

CHOCOLATE AND ORANGE WHITE POPPY SEED BREAD

White poppy seeds, or khus khus, are used to add texture and a nutty flavor to mithai. I used the white poppy seeds similarly to how black poppy seeds are used in lemon poppy seed bread. You can find white poppy seeds at your local Indian store or on Amazon.

MAKES
1 (9 X 5-INCH [23 X 13-CM]) LOAF

CHOCOLATE AND ORANGE WHITE POPPY SEED BREAD

1¼ cups (283 g) unsalted butter, room temperature, plus more for greasing

1⅓ cups (166 g) all-purpose flour

½ cup (43 g) unsweetened cocoa powder

1 tsp salt

¼ cup (28 g) white poppy seeds

1 cup plus 1 tbsp (215 g) granulated sugar

2 tbsp (12 g) orange zest

4 eggs

1 egg yolk

1 tsp vanilla extract

2 tbsp (30 ml) fresh orange juice

ORANGE ICING

1½ cups (180 g) powdered sugar

1 tbsp (15 ml) fresh orange juice

Preheat the oven to 325°F (163°C). Grease a 9 x 5-inch (23 x 13-cm) loaf pan with a little butter and set aside.

In a small bowl, whisk together the flour, cocoa powder, salt and white poppy seeds. Set aside.

In a mixing bowl, add the sugar and orange zest. Rub the sugar and zest together with your fingers until the sugar turns a pale orange color. This will help the cake get a stronger orange flavor as the oils in the zest are released while you rub it into the sugar. Cream the butter for 5 minutes until pale and fluffy. Add the eggs and egg yolk one at a time, mixing well in between each addition. Add the vanilla and fresh orange juice and mix for 1 minute. Add the dry ingredients to the wet batter and mix until just combined. Use a spatula to fold the mixture to make sure there are no pockets of flour anywhere. Spoon the mixture into the greased loaf pan and smooth out into an even layer.

Bake for 50 to 60 minutes, turning the pan 180 degrees halfway through baking. The bread is done when a toothpick inserted in the middle comes out clean. Once done, let the bread cool for 15 minutes in the pan and then turn the bread out and cool completely on a rack.

To make the orange icing, whisk together the powdered sugar and orange juice until you have a smooth icing. Drizzle the icing over the cooled bread. Let the icing set for 10 minutes and serve!

PEAR AND CARDAMOM SCONES

These pear and cardamom scones are my way of giving a nod to India's British past. Similar to most baked goods in India, I took a British classic and added additional spices to give it my own little twist. These scones would be perfect for a fancy afternoon tea party!

MAKES
8 SCONES

2¾ cups (344 g) all-purpose flour, plus more for baking sheet

2¼ tsp (10 g) baking powder

1¼ tsp (3 g) ground cardamom

¼ tsp of salt

3 tbsp (42 g) dark brown sugar

½ cup (113 g) unsalted butter, cold, cut into 1-inch (2.5-cm) cubes

2 eggs

1 tsp vanilla extract

3 tbsp (45 ml) date syrup or maple syrup

2 tbsp (30 ml) heavy cream, plus additional to brush on

2 medium Bartlett pears, peeled and diced into ½-inch (1-cm) cubes

ICING

2 tbsp (30 ml) date syrup or maple syrup

½ cup (60 g) powdered sugar

Preheat the oven to 400°F (204°C). Line a baking sheet with parchment paper.

In a large bowl, add the flour, baking powder, cardamom, salt and brown sugar. Whisk well. Add the cold, cubed butter and use your hands or a pastry cutter to rub the butter into the dry ingredients until it is a sandy texture. Add the eggs, vanilla, date syrup and heavy cream. Bring the mixture together into a rough dough. Add in the pears and mix in. The dough should be slightly dry and crumbly, and come together into a dough ball if you squeeze a fistful together. If it feels too dry, add 1 tablespoon (15 ml) additional heavy cream, and if it's too wet, add 1 tablespoon (8 g) of flour.

Sprinkle the parchment-lined baking sheet with some flour and gather the dough into the center of the baking tray. Use your hands to mold the dough into a circle that is ½ inch (1 cm) thick. Use a knife to cut the dough into eight triangles/wedges. Use a spatula to separate the scones so that there is a 1-inch (2.5-cm) gap between each scone. Brush each scone lightly with the heavy cream. Bake the scones for 12 to 14 minutes, or until the tops are golden brown. Cool the scones on a rack.

To make the icing, add the date syrup and powdered sugar to a bowl and mix well. Drizzle the icing onto the scones and let them set. Enjoy with a cup of tea or coffee!

PEACH AND GINGER PUFF PASTRIES

Spice up your next brunch with these peach puff pastries that have just a hint of ginger. Peach and ginger pair really well together and make a delicious strudel-esque pastry. To save time, I used store-bought puff pastry, but if you are up for the challenge and have some time, I say go for it!

MAKES
9 PASTRIES

2 large peaches

1 tbsp (15 ml) honey

½ tbsp (8 g) granulated sugar

2 tsp (4 g) ginger, minced

1 (10 x 15–inch [25 x 38–cm]) sheet of puff pastry

1 egg, beaten

2 tbsp (20 g) slivered almonds

ICING
¼ cup (30 g) powdered sugar

¾ tsp milk

¼ tsp vanilla extract

Preheat the oven to 400°F (204°C). Line a baking sheet with parchment paper.

Slice the peaches into ½-inch (1-cm)-thick slices and place into a bowl. Add the honey, granulated sugar and ginger and toss well. Set aside for 10 minutes. Place the puff pastry sheet onto the parchment-lined baking sheet. Cut the puff pastry into nine squares. Use a spatula to separate out the puff pastry so that there are 2 inches (5 cm) between each piece.

Divide the peaches evenly amongst the nine squares and place them in a diagonal line. Fold the opposite corners over each other in the center of the peaches. Brush the exposed puff pastry with the beaten egg and sprinkle the slivered almonds over the top of each pastry. Bake for 20 to 25 minutes or until golden brown. Cool completely.

To make the icing, add the powdered sugar, milk and vanilla to a small bowl and mix until smooth. Drizzle the icing on top of the pastries and let the icing set for 15 minutes before serving.

GREEN MANGO MARMALADE (CHHUNDO)

Chhundo is a savory sweet marmalade made with shredded green mango. It's a popular accompaniment to dinner in Gujarat. It's typically made by tossing shredded mango with sugar and salt and then placing the mixture into a jar to set in the sun for a couple of days, until most of the liquid has evaporated and you're left with a sticky marmalade. My family still makes it this way in the summer, but here is a quick stovetop version that is just as good! It's a great addition to your breakfast toast or to a cheese board for a party.

MAKES
1 CUP (240 ML) CHHUNDO

2 cups (321 g) unripe green mango, grated

½ tbsp (9 g) salt

1 cup (200 g) granulated sugar

1 (½-inch [1-cm]) piece cinnamon stick

¼ tsp cardamom seeds

1 tsp red chili powder, or to taste

Add the grated mango and salt to a saucepan. Stir well and let this rest for 5 minutes. Add the granulated sugar to the mango mixture and stir well so that the sugar is well incorporated. Let the mixture rest for 10 minutes. Cook over medium-high heat for 15 minutes, or until most of the liquid evaporates, stirring continuously. Remove from the heat and stir in the cinnamon, cardamom and chili powder. Spoon into a clean jar and close with the lid. Cool completely on the counter. Once cool, keep in the refrigerator for up to 3 months.

APRICOT MURRABA (KHUBANI KI MURRABA)

Murrabas are fruit preserves that were brought to India by the Persians. There are many versions of murrabas all across the Middle East and Asia, but apricot murraba, or khubani ki murraba, is popular in India and Pakistan. This apricot jam is spiced with cardamom and is wonderful with almond butter in sandwiches!

MAKES
2½ CUPS (613 G)

½ cup (100 g) granulated sugar

½ cup (114 g) brown sugar

1 cup (240 ml) water

½ tsp cardamom seeds, slightly crushed

¼ tsp salt

9 apricots (453 g), pitted and quartered

Add the granulated sugar, brown sugar, water, cardamom and salt to a heavy-bottomed saucepan over medium-low heat. When the sugar is dissolved and the mixture starts to boil, add the quartered apricots and stir well. Simmer over low heat for 40 minutes. You can test if the jam is ready by placing a plate in the freezer for 10 minutes and then dropping a small amount (about the size of a dime) of the jam onto the plate. After a couple seconds, if the jam sets, it's ready! If the jam is still runny, then keep simmering and test again in 5 minutes. Once the jam is done, pour into a clean jar and screw on the lid. Let it cool completely on the counter. Once cool, keep in the refrigerator for up to 3 months.

DRINKS

If you walk into any Indian home, the first thing you will be offered is "chai pani." It's ingrained in Indian hospitality to believe that "atithi devo bhava," guests are like God, and to treat them with respect. That starts with offering either a cool drink or a hot cup of chai. Beverages in India are usually made with a mixture of spices added to a milk or juice base, making each drink unique. Every region (and family) has their own masala or mix of spices they like to use.

A lot of drinks stem from ancient Ayurvedic practices. For example, nimbu pani (Masala Limeade [page 160]) has ingredients in it that have natural cooling effects on the body, and is given out during blistering hot summer days. Masala Chai (page 156) was invented by fusing an unpalatable Ayurvedic drink made with ground spices and sweetened milky black tea.

The drink recipes in this chapter are directly from my mom's kitchen. Each recipe is personal to every family, so feel free to change and add ingredients to make these drinks a part of yours!

MASALA CHAI

Every family has their own recipe for masala chai. There are so many changeable factors when making tea. For example, the type of tea (loose or tea bags), the amount of sugar, the ratio of spices or the ratio of milk to water in the chai can all be changed to suit your preference. Even how long the tea is steeped changes from family to family. This isn't the definitive recipe for masala chai, but it is in my family!

MAKES
2 TO 4 SERVINGS

⅓ cup (80 ml) water

1½ tbsp (6 g) black tea (preferably CTC)

1 tbsp (15 g) granulated sugar, or to taste

4 whole cloves

2-inch (5-cm) piece of cinnamon

½ tsp cardamom seeds, coarsely crushed

2 star anise pods

1 tbsp (2.5 g) fresh ginger, minced

2 cups (480 ml) milk

Add the water, tea and granulated sugar to a small saucepan. Bring to a boil. Add the cloves, cinnamon, cardamom, star anise and ginger to the saucepan and stir. Simmer for 1 minute. Add the milk. Bring the chai to a boil over medium heat. It'll quickly simmer up the sides of the pan, so don't take your eyes off of it! Stir occasionally until the milk simmers up the pan, about 4 minutes. Turn the heat down immediately. Once the milk settles, turn the heat up slightly and let the chai come up to a simmer. Remove from the heat. Strain into a mug or teacup and enjoy!

NOTE: Pair this masala chai with Thandai Cake Rusks (page 85), Nankhatai (page 88) or Khari Biscuits (page 92).

STRAWBERRY LASSI

You can make lassi out of any fruit and yogurt mixture, but the most famous is mango and yogurt. I prefer strawberry and banana lassi for a healthy morning breakfast that is quick and easy to make!

MAKES
2 TO 4 SERVINGS

4 cups (283 g) whole strawberries

1 medium banana

1½ cups (340 g) plain Greek yogurt

2 tbsp (30 ml) agave syrup, honey or your choice of liquid sweetener

½ tsp ground cardamom

Pinch of salt

Chopped pistachios, for garnish

Wash and cut the tops off all of the strawberries and add them to a blender. Add the peeled banana, yogurt, agave syrup, cardamom and salt. Blend until smooth. Pour into glasses and garnish with the chopped pistachios.

MASALA LIMEADE

Nimbu pani, aka masala limeade, is my absolute favorite drink! Fennel and cumin have naturally cooling properties, and the black salt adds a tartness and savoriness that I can't get enough of. This drink is perfect to cool off with on a hot summer day, but also great for when you have an upset stomach. This drink was my mom's version of Gatorade for me when I was growing up, and is a great way to get electrolytes back into your system after an upset stomach!

MAKES
4 TO 6 SERVINGS

1 tsp fennel seeds

1 tsp cumin seeds

½ cup (120 ml) fresh lime juice

3 tbsp (45 g) granulated sugar

1 tbsp (15 ml) agave syrup (or any other liquid sweetener)

½ tsp black salt (kala namak)

1 tsp ground black pepper

4 cups (960 ml) water

10 mint leaves

1 lime, cut in wedges

Toast the fennel and cumin seeds in a small skillet over medium heat for 1 minute, stirring often. Pour the seeds into a spice blender and blend until you have a coarse powder. If you don't have a spice blender, use a mortar and pestle to coarsely crush the spices.

Add the lime juice, granulated sugar, agave, black salt, pepper, cumin and fennel powder and water to a large bowl. Mix well and let sit for 10 to 15 minutes.

Muddle the mint in a large pitcher. Strain the masala limeade into the pitcher. To serve, pour the masala limeade into ice-filled glasses and garnish with lime wedges and mint.

NOTE: Indian black salt, or kala namak, can be found at your local Indian store or on Amazon. It's actually pink in color, not black. It has a unique sulfuric taste, which is why black salt does such a great job mimicking eggs in vegan omelette recipes! I like to sprinkle it on popcorn, apples or cucumbers.

SAPOTA (CHIKOO) MILKSHAKE

Chikoo (also known as sapota or sapodilla) is a round, brown fruit native to Central America. It was brought over to South Asia in the early 1800s by the Portuguese. It has an earthy, caramel-y brown sugar flavor with a gritty pear-like texture and gives this milkshake a salted caramel flavor. You can find chikoo in the frozen aisle at Latin/Hispanic and Indian grocery stores.

MAKES
4 TO 6 SERVINGS

WHIPPED CREAM
¼ cup (60 ml) heavy whipping cream

1 tbsp (8 g) powdered sugar

½ tsp vanilla extract

MILKSHAKE
2 cups (248 g) sapota (chikoo), fresh or frozen

2 cups (480 ml) milk (nut, dairy or coconut)

1½ cups (353 g) vanilla ice cream

4 Medjool dates, pitted

2 tbsp (20 g) raw cashews

¼ tsp cardamom seeds

½ tsp salt

Add the heavy whipping cream, powdered sugar and vanilla to a large, cold bowl. Use a hand mixer to whip the cream until you get stiff peaks. Set aside.

Add the chikoo, milk, ice cream, dates, cashews, cardamom and salt to a blender. Blend until the milkshake is smooth. Pour the milkshake into tall glasses and top with the whipped cream. Serve immediately.

JAGGERY LEMON ICED TEA

A cold refreshing drink perfect for a hot summer day. This iced tea is sweetened with jaggery and can be likened to Southern sweet tea.

MAKES
2 TO 4 SERVINGS

2 cups (480 ml) water, divided

¼ cup (36 g) jaggery, or to taste

2 tea bags of black tea

4 tbsp (60 ml) fresh lemon juice

Add 1 cup (240 ml) of water and the jaggery to a small saucepan over medium heat and bring to a boil. Once the water boils, remove from the heat and add the tea bags. Steep the tea for 2 to 5 minutes, depending on how strong you want your iced tea to be. Stir in the rest of the water and lemon juice. Strain the tea into ice-filled glasses.

ORANGE, POMEGRANATE AND ROSE SHARBAT

Sharbat is a drink made with a concentration of fruit juices mixed with water. My family would make sharbat during special occasions or parties. We always mixed fruit juices, almost like cocktails or fruit punch. This sharbat is amazing on its own or with a splash of gin!

MAKES
2 TO 4 SERVINGS

1½ tbsp (14 g) jaggery powder

1 tbsp (15 g) granulated sugar

1 tbsp (15 ml) honey

⅓ cup (80 ml) orange juice

1 cup (240 ml) 100% pomegranate juice, divided

2 cups (480 ml) water, divided

¼ tsp rose water

Add the jaggery powder, granulated sugar, honey, orange juice, ½ cup (120 ml) of pomegranate juice and ½ cup (120 ml) of water into a small saucepan over medium-high heat. Bring the mixture to a boil and then simmer over low heat for 15 minutes. Cool for 5 minutes. Stir in ½ cup (120 ml) of pomegranate juice, 1½ cups (360 ml) of water and rose water. Stir well and pour into ice-filled glasses to serve.

WATERMELON AND BASIL SEED SHARBAT

Basil seeds, or takmaria, are found in various Asian and Middle Eastern drinks. They are usually touted for their health benefits and are added to drinks for texture. They have a jelly-like and crunchy texture that people either love or hate. If you're feeling adventurous, try this unique sharbat!

MAKES
4 TO 6 SERVINGS

2 tsp plus 2 tbsp (16 g) basil seeds, divided

1½ cups (360 ml) water, divided

4 cups (608 g) watermelon, diced

1 tbsp (15 ml) lime juice

2 tbsp (30 g) granulated sugar, or to taste

Add 2 teaspoons (4 g) of basil seeds and ½ cup (120 ml) of water to a small bowl and set aside for 10 minutes. The basil seeds will swell and a thin layer of jelly will form around each seed. Add the watermelon, remaining water, lime juice and sugar to a blender and blend until completely smooth. Strain the juice into ice-filled glasses. Stir in 1 tablespoon (6 g) of the basil seeds into each cup and serve.

ACKNOWLEDGMENTS

This book could not have been written without the influence of my mother and the women of my family. They spent years perfecting their recipes and sharing them with the next generation and for that, I am thankful. Thank you to my husband and daughter for being my official taste testers and always being honest with your feedback. Rhut, I wouldn't have been able to follow my dreams and make this happen if it wasn't for you. Thank you for seeing the passion in me and pushing me to pursue a career in the food industry. I am so very lucky to have found someone who encourages me and gives me confidence to do what I love. To my sister, Deepti, thank you for spending hours on FaceTime with me to go over book ideas and editing my first draft. I am so very lucky to have you. To my dad, thank you for coming to America and giving me the chance at living a life full of passion and opportunities. I couldn't have asked for a better taste tester than you!

Also, a big thank you to my recipe testers: Aparna Kothary, Madhumita Mukundab, Molly Tullis, Trishala Parthasarathi, Priyanka Patel, Smruti Ashar, Kavya Dathathreya, Tahmeena, Pranjal Boghara, Surabhi Maheshwari, Priyam Shah, Katie Frazell, Avani Shah, Jesmine La Russa, Meera Patel, Arpita Patel, Shana Bull, Amy Patel, Malika Rajvanshy, Payal Shah, Daniela Djayaputra and Faye Rodriguez. Without you, this book could not have been written. Thank you for taking time to make my recipes in your kitchens and making sure that this cookbook wasn't a complete mess!

Last but not least, thank you to all of the people who have touched my life: you've left an imprint with me whether you know it or not.

ABOUT THE AUTHOR

Hetal Vasavada is the food blogger and recipe developer behind Milk & Cardamom. She is a former healthcare consultant and *MasterChef* Season 6 contestant. She founded her own marketing consulting firm where she aids startups with recipe development, business development, social media and content creation. She is a New Jersey native who has adopted the beautiful city of San Francisco as home. You can find Hetal wandering the farmers' market near her home with her husband chasing after their two-year-old daughter.

INDEX